a fine line

a fine line

how design strategies are shaping the future of business

hartmut esslinger

founder of frog design

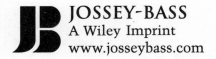

JOSSEY-BASS
A Wiley Imprint
www.josseybass.com

Published by Jossey-Bass
A Wiley Imprint
989 Market Street, San Francisco, CA 94103-1741—www.josseybass.com

Jossey-Bass books and products are available through most bookstores. To contact Jossey-Bass directly call our Customer Care Department within the U.S. at 800-956-7739, outside the U.S. at 317-572-3986, or fax 317-572-4002.

Jossey-Bass also publishes its books in a variety of electronic formats. Some content that appears in print may not be available in electronic books.

Library of Congress Cataloging-in-Publication Data

Esslinger, Hartmut
  A fine line : how design strategies are shaping the future of
business / Hartmut Esslinger. — 1st ed.
    p. cm.
  Includes bibliographical references and index.
  ISBN 978-0-470-45102-1 (cloth)
  1. Industrial design. 2. New products. I. Title.
  TS171.E85 2009
  658.5'75—dc22

                                        2009011951

Printed in the United States of America
FIRST EDITION
HB Printing   10 9 8 7 6 5 4 3 2 1

contents

v

With gratitude to

my wife and partner Patricia Roller,

my children Marc, Nico, Max, & Anna
(she gave this book its title),

my teacher Karl Dittert,

my first client Dieter Motte,

my friends inside and outside of frog design,

my world-challenging students,

and my courageous clients.

foreword

Decades ago, when the Apple II temporarily ruled the computing landscape, I was in the passenger seat of a Mercedes being driven by Steve Jobs along the hilly roads above Woodside, California. Steve was extolling the virtues of the user interface embodied in the car's window controls when he suddenly started to talk about an extraordinary industrial designer he had just visited in Bavaria who insisted on driving at breakneck speed. That man was Hartmut Esslinger.

Many years later, through one of those odd quirks of fate, I found myself sitting on the board of Flextronics at the time that it acquired Hartmut's company, frog design. Yet it was only when I read this book that I came to realize all the places that bear Hartmut's fingerprints. Many people know of the breakthrough work he did for Sony and Apple. Far fewer know that his mark also lies on the ergonomic design of a line of equipment for dentists' offices; the first-class compartments of Lufthansa airplanes; the logo for Windows; and exquisite Louis Vuitton goods.

Hartmut's book contains the ruminations of a man who has devoted his life to the challenge of marrying the aesthetic with the functional while standing firm against the deadening forces of mediocrity. His work shows that taste can triumph, design and production can be soul-mates, and the eye of an individual can shape a product and a company. The idea that finely designed products can change the fate of companies while also becoming our indispensable companions is a message that millions of us owe to Hartmut.

Michael Moritz
Partner, Sequoia Capital

about hartmut esslinger

A native of Beuren, Germany, Hartmut Esslinger founded frog design in 1969, when he was just twenty-five years old, and quickly developed the company into one of the world's leading strategic design firms. Hartmut pioneered the use of design as a means of humanizing technology. His stylish, elegant, and user-friendly designs revolutionized the look and functionality of computer systems, consumer electronics, and other high-tech products and equipment. His contributions to Apple's "Snow White" design language resulted in the ground-breaking Apple II computer series, which earned *Time* magazine's Design of the Year award in 1984 and established Apple's identity as a trend-setting, user-oriented brand. Over the past forty years, working with his partner and wife, Patricia Roller, Hartmut has contributed to the success of numerous other global firms, including Acer, Adidas, AT&T, CitiCorp, Dell, Disney, GE, Hewlett-Packard, Honda, IBM, Kodak, Louis Vuitton, Microsoft, Motor-ola, MTV, SAP, Siemens, Sony, Sun Microsystems, Swatch, Virgin Mobile, Yahoo!, and Yamaha, to name only a few. In 1990, *BusinessWeek* maga-zine named him the most influential American industrial designer since the 1930s and the first "Superstar of High-Tech Design." Esslinger has received several hundred design and innovation awards and an honorary

Doctorate in Fine Arts from Parsons the New School for Design. His work holds a place in the permanent collection of New York's Museum of Modern Art, the Smithsonian Institute, and Neue Sammlung in Munich.

Since leaving his role as co-CEO of frog design in 2006, Hartmut has remained active as an educator and innovator. He is a founding professor of the Hochschule fuer Gestaltung (College for Design) in Karlsruhe, Germany, and a professor for convergent industrial design at the University for Applied Arts in Vienna, Austria.

Today frog design is one of the world's foremost global innovation firms, helping companies create and bring to market meaningful products, services, and experiences. With a team of more than four hundred designers, technologists, strategists, and analysts, the company delivers fully convergent experiences that span multiple technologies, platforms, and media. frog works across a broad spectrum of industries, including consumer electronics, telecommunications, healthcare, media, education, finance, retail, and fashion. Headquartered in San Francisco, frog has offices in Austin, New York, San Jose, Seattle, Milan, Amsterdam, Stuttgart, and Shanghai. frog is an independent division of Aricent, a global innovation, technology, and outsourcing company, owned by Kohlberg Kravis Roberts & Co., Sequoia Capital, The Family Office, and Flextronics.

frog has won numerous awards, including *BusinessWeek* IDEA, Red Dot Design, *I.D.* magazine, and IF awards, and its work has been featured extensively by media, analysts, and researchers. frog speaks at conferences worldwide and publishes the award-winning *design mind* publication. The company has helped launch the Designers Accord, an industry-wide program to establish sustainable principles for design firms, and it serves on the advisory board of Design Ignites Change, an initiative that promotes design thinking among students. frog also partners with Pop!Tech, a social innovation network, to support entrepreneurs with incubating businesses in emerging markets.

introduction

"Do something wonderful, people may imitate it."
—ALBERT SCHWEITZER

Where does creativity come from? Neurologists, artists, and many others have offered plenty of answers to that question, but I think we are born with the seeds of creativity within us. It's up to us to discover, develop, and defend our gifts and prove that we deserve them. As a very young man, coming of age during the social and economic upheavals that rocked post-World War II Germany, I had to make some difficult but necessary choices about how I would defend and develop my own creative gift—choices that began with a painful family rift and led to a rich and satisfying career as a designer, entrepreneur, innovator, global business strategist, and educator. Making those choices, I stepped over the fine line that sometimes separates creativity from comfort to found my own firm, frog design, which stands today as one of the world's innovation leaders. This book explores the adventure that followed, as I learned to navigate and then chart new waters in collaborative business design. I've written this book as a guide to that process, with the goal of encouraging business leaders and designers to join forces in building creative strategies for a more profitable and sustainable future.

As the most successful companies and brands know, design isn't just about making something look good. Design enables a company to invent and project innovative concepts that enhance human interactions and experiences. And, when we design a new and better object or a more inspiring human experience, the design itself becomes a branding symbol. People recognize visual symbols as cultural expression, and we embrace those symbols that reflect our deeper values, such as a delight in simple, elegant usability. In essence, design humanizes technology and helps businesses appeal to the human spirit. And it is the cultural context of design that roots business in history and connects it to a more profound future.

I have been successful in life because I understood very early on that business needs creativity like humans need oxygen, and I was able to convince my clients that they needed to "breathe" in order to flourish. It hasn't been easy. In the beginning I knew that, as both a consumer and a designer, I wanted technical products that were designed to connect with people on an emotional level, an idea I would later sum up as "emotional design." Those kinds of products weren't being manufactured in my native homeland, Germany, nor in many other places back in the 1960s when I started my company. Forty years later, frog design has had an impact on manufacturing and service industry offerings around the world, and the design-driven strategies of global brands such as Sony, Apple, Microsoft, SAP, Motorola, HP, and GE carry the frog DNA.

I am fortunate to have spent my professional life creating successful design-driven strategies with these dynamic corporations. Having learned firsthand how truly great business leaders partner with designers, I have developed a step-by-step innovation process that leverages the power of that partnership. That process is at the heart of the collaborative model of innovation-driven business design that I've outlined in this book. Each chapter details a critical phase of the successful innovation-driven business strategy, illustrated with ideas, strategies, and stories aimed at informing designers and business leaders, alike.

First, we'll examine the role of design in the rapidly developing creative economy and how savvy business leaders cultivate a culture of innovation within their organizations. With the buy-in from management in place, we'll tackle the real challenges and rewards of forming winning business design strategies before making plans for their tactical implementation. Next, we'll walk through a step-by-step overview of the innovation process, from targeting goals to successfully shepherding innovations to market, and then take an in-depth look at the tools of innovation and the sometimes counterintuitive process of following a highly technical path to arrive at an intensely human experience. We'll explore the growing and urgent demand for business strategies based on environmental sustainability, and the role of those strategies in the future of a thriving, lasting global economy. From developing early stage solutions for "green" consumer products and experiences to adopting global collaborative design processes, the examples of frog's successful design-driven innovations discussed in this book offer critical insights into the process of crafting business models that can establish a foothold in the new, green economy. Finally, we'll take a long look at the future of manufacturing and how businesses can transform the "cheap, cheaper, toxic" model of production outsourcing into one of mutually beneficial economic and industrial collaboration. Together, these chapters form a working guide to the process of infusing any business with the creative energy of design-driven innovation.

Throughout this book, I've woven bits and pieces of my personal and professional history. I've included these stories, in part, to offer an insider's look at the creative life. More importantly, however, I wanted to give readers a rare opportunity to sit around the planning desk with some of the world-class business leaders I've worked with during my career—some of the brightest business minds of our age, including Dieter Motte, Akio Morita, and Norio Ohga of Sony, Henri Racamier of Louis Vuitton, Hasso Plattner of SAP, and yes, Steve Jobs of Apple.

Today, the business world is going through a period of profound and massive change that goes far deeper than falling stock markets and drops in consumer spending. The markets of efficiency—based on a ruthless quest for lower costs, no matter the social, environmental, or economic damage—are giving way to a new, creative economy. Customization and niche markets are eroding the demand for mass-produced commodities, and businesses are looking for ways to connect with their customers on an emotional level. Environmental sustainability, once ignored by many businesses, has become the new mantra for any enterprise looking for a secure foothold in 21st century markets. Around the world, business leaders are turning to designers to help create a strategy that will define their brand, by appealing to consumers' emotions, providing rewarding consumer experiences, and building an environmentally responsible approach to doing business.

In the end, the business-design partnership advances our industrial culture by providing sustainable innovation, cultural identity, and economic consistency. But to accomplish that goal, design must cross the line that separates commercial-functional benchmarks from cultural relevance and spirituality. This book examines that fine line as it courses through our material culture, distinguishing "great" from "good," creative strategies from imitative acts, and excellence from also-ran mediocrity.

In my experience, true success comes for the designer and the business executive when the two can bridge the artificial lines that too often have separated their worlds. This book also talks about building that bridge—about how creative minds and business minds collaborate, and how both sides of the business-design partnership can prosper within that process. I won't say that this collaboration is a silver bullet for every problem facing a company, but I do believe it is the best way to develop a better business today and to build a sustainable future for that business. I've written this book to promote and inspire a new business reality. The stories and ideas in these pages offer proof that the cultural, humanistic, and economic power of creative design is better for the bottom line, better for business, and better for our planet as a whole.

a fine line

design-driven strategy
staking a claim in the creative economy

"To be is to do."
—IMMANUEL KANT

It's a big leap for a creative consulting company to grow from its roots in a tiny garage in Germany's Black Forest to a position of influence with esteemed global franchises, but I see the story of that transition as just one example of the incredible power of the business/design alliance. Today, there's much talk about the "new" power of this alliance, but the power of design-driven business strategy isn't a new idea at all. It's the idea that spurred me to start my own design firm in 1969, and it's what drove Steve Jobs to hire my firm to join him in building such a strategy for his own company. What's new is the rapidly growing recognition of this power and the need for cultivating it. A first step toward achieving that goal is a firm understanding of the vital role of design in shaping an innovation-driven business model.

When I founded my design firm, my goals were simple, yet powerful: to redefine design as a strategic profession, and to continually promote its relevance to industry and business. I wanted to create technical

1

products that consumers could love for their beauty and their usefulness. And I wanted all designers, including myself, to be masters of our own destiny, not just hired hands brought in to put a shining new face on the same, tired old ideas. I was determined to bring my ideas to the world—and I felt as though every moment of my life had been spent in preparation for that opportunity.

Because I grew up in war-torn Germany, a country still coming to grips with the atrocities of the Third Reich, my aesthetic and my ideologies could not help but be informed by the changing world around me. I was born on June 5, 1944, in Beuren, a tiny village buried deep in Germany's Black Forest. The only adult men under the age of sixty in my village were French soldiers who had occupied the area—all of our fathers and older brothers had died in the war or were being held in POW camps. Too young to really understand the concept of war, we children always tried to listen to adults when they spoke in hushed tones about "the bombings" and "Stalingrad," but none of it made much sense to us. No one spoke of the Nazi terror or the Third Reich—not even my extended family, which, as I learned many years later, had lost seven of its own members to the concentration camps.

When our men eventually did come home from the camps—my father, Johannes Heinrich Esslinger, among them—they were strangers to us. These silent, brooding men spoke little about the war or their experiences in it, but their bursts of rage and violence could be triggered by the merest childhood prank and often ended in beatings for us children. Sometimes, we guiltily found ourselves envying friends who had lost their fathers and were treated that much better by their grieving mothers. Years later, a group of American officers came to my school and showed us students a documentary film about the war, some of the footage shot by the Nazis themselves and some taken by the Allies as they liberated the concentration camps. As I grasped the reality of what had unfolded in my country during the war, I was enveloped in shame, sadness, and fury, and a new understanding of the bitter forces that had shaped my father and his fellow soldiers. "Never again, Fascism!" I thought to myself. Better to be a rebellious outcast than a blindly obedient servant.

Yet even in these dark, uncertain early years, my youth was influenced by beauty as well as war. As Germany began to rebuild its industrial infrastructure after the war, my parents started a small business in textiles and, on my tenth birthday, we moved to the small town of Altensteig. There my parents bought a live-in commercial space downtown, where they opened a clothing store. That move brought aesthetics into my life on a daily basis. I was surrounded by nice clothes, the latest fashion magazines, and visiting fashion shows, not to mention an ever-changing parade of attractive and exotic fashion models.

By the time I entered high school, my creative drive had emerged. Whenever I saw a car—still an oddity in my small village—I drew it, and eventually filled countless notebooks with sketches of cars, motorcycles, and ships, all of my own design. My mother, seeing the drawings as a waste of time and a warning sign of future social decline, burned my sketchbooks, declaring "All artists end up in the gutter," as I watched the bright pages of my notebooks curl up and turn to ash in the family hearth. After high school, I joined the German army and then entered school to train as an engineer, but even my commanders and professors understood that my creative energies and interests were driving me toward a different future than their training could provide. Eventually, I was forced to choose between my parents' goals for my life and my own. I chose to pursue a life in design.

I entered the College of Design in Schwäbisch Gmünd, Germany (today one of the world's top-ten design schools), and there, on a summer night in 1968, my life changed. I had gathered that evening with my fellow students to compete in a design contest sponsored by the Kienzle Clock Company. My entry was a proposal for a radio watch capable of displaying the radio signal from the atomic clock in Braunschweig, and I had great hopes of winning the first-place prize money. But the jurors—including Kienzle's chief designer—viciously criticized all of the student designs as being "unrealistic" and refused to grant the first-place prize to any of us. One of the jurors even picked up some of the models, shook them in the air, then threw the pieces on the ground. (Today, of course, radio watches are an industry standard. My "unrealistic" concept became a product for the German watchmaker Junghans; the watch is still considered to be the most accurate commercially available clock in the world.)

This short-sighted, quick rejection offered me a much greater incentive to succeed as a designer than any trophy or prize money would have done. On the drive home that night, I swore that I would change the world of design by transforming its stuffy, hierarchical limits into something more dynamic, where anything is possible. I determined that the only way to liberate myself from the unimaginative and outmoded design model imposed by the "Kienzle Clock Companies" of the world was to start my own business. It was the most optimistic and radical step I could ever take.

o the business of design

And so, in 1969, while still a student, I started "esslinger design"—the firm that would become frog. The first goal I set for myself was to achieve economic success. I refused to accept the role of the starving artist. Besides, I was certain that the design process was too important to be ignored by companies looking to gain a strong competitive advantage, and I knew there were business leaders out there who would value the profession as much as I did. The rest of the plan was simple but ambitious, and I wrote it down in six steps:

1. Look for "hungry" clients who want to go to the top;
2. Be business-minded and do great work for my clients, not for myself;
3. Get famous—not as an egotistic artist, but as a visionary;
4. Use that fame as working capital to build the company;
5. Build the best global design company ever; and
6. Always look for the best people—as employees, partners, and clients.

After two years, Andreas Haug and Georg Spreng joined me as my first partners. One day we were sitting around our coffee table, and Andreas asked, "What are our plans for the future?" "To have an esslinger-designed product in each of the major shopping centers on earth," I shot back. Everybody laughed, but seven years later my seemingly grandiose plan had become a reality.

My first step toward that goal came soon. I had always been interested in electronics—as an amateur jazz and rock musician I had built my own amplifiers from mail-order components. I also was very fond of a small consumer electronics brand called Wega, a company that had been founded in the 1920s. When my first diploma semester came up in 1968, my project of choice was to design a portable radio with speakers that folded in for compact storage, but provided true stereo sound when opened out. While working on this design, I heard rumors that Wega's owner and CEO, Dieter Motte, was looking for a new signature designer. So I called him and asked for an interview. He was an extremely nice man, and a total design fanatic, with the strategic goal of positioning Wega as a design brand with an appeal that extended beyond the "elitists." He liked my work and admired my engineering background, and so he offered me an internship. But that wasn't what I was shooting for.

Shortly after our meeting, I read that the German federal government had announced the first "Bundespreis Gute Form" (Federal Design Award), to be awarded in 1969. With an updated version of my diploma project, I won the student award, a huge coup for any young designer. The ceremony was held in Berlin as part of the German Industrial Fair, and I was presented my award by Germany's Secretary of Finance and Trade Karl Schiller. As it happened, Dieter Motte also was in the audience, and after the ceremony he came to me and simply said ". . . sorry that I underestimated you, but we have to work together!" These words launched a great relationship, and my professional career.

Working out of the garage of a rented house, I came up with the concept for our first big initiative—Wega's System 3000, which combined a television set with high-end stereo components. Taking advantage of innovations in plastics manufacturing, our design pioneered the use of plastic-bodied stereo components with foam-encased electronic elements. The results were far more aesthetically pleasing, functional, modern, and pounds lighter than the traditional wood and plywood-encased stereos that dominated the market at that time. I designed the System 3000 like a sculpture, so that it looked great from every angle (its surface texture of graduated, embossed dots served as the inspiration for this book's cover design).

We introduced our prototype at the Consumer Electronics Show in Berlin in 1971. After the show, the System 3000 took off and I was flooded with new work from Wega and from other clients, both large and small. In 1973, Dieter Motte's family began looking for a buyer, and so I accepted an offer from Sony in November of that year. Then, in January of 1974, Sony bought the Wega company, and I was on my way to Japan—the consultant of a massive, global corporation. The frog was flying.

Just after the sale of Wega to Sony, I met Hans-Otto Doering, the co-owner of *FORM* magazine, which at the time was the most popular design magazine in Germany. We were finally successful enough to afford a bit of advertising, and Hans-Otto and I met in front of my garage shop to talk about ad possibilities in his magazine. He tried to sell me some space on an inside page, but I asked for the "prime real estate" of the back cover. He looked at me skeptically, and asked if I was sure that our tiny garage-based operation could afford to carry such an expensive ad place- ment for a guaranteed time. "Yes," I said. "Why not?" Hans-Otto shook his head in disbelief, but we signed a contract on the top of a trash can— and cemented a relationship that would last thirty-three years.

With the back cover of *FORM,* our tiny company began to take shape in the public eye. We bought a Brazilian tree frog, photographed it in an outrageously funny jumping session, and published it in our back page ad. Not long after that we adopted a green frog as our logo—we felt it was a fitting image, given the vast numbers of frogs that inhabited our native Black Forest, and that the word "frog" itself is hidden in our country's name—the (F)ederal (R)epublic (O)f (G)ermany ("frog design" is always printed in lower-case, a rebellion against German grammatical rules that, forty years later, other companies are beginning to adopt). As the com- pany grew, we refined our ads to be as seductive, attention-getting, and innovative as possible. We saw our firm as an alternative to the big and boring names that dominated the industry at that time, and we wanted to position ourselves as such. Taking those back covers forced us to define our message and to create a strategy of self-promotion around it. We ambitiously declared ourselves "the new face of German-Global design."

Today, frog helps its clients create defendable, multi-billion-dollar yearly revenues, and frog-designed products, media solutions, and experiences are everywhere. "With a little help from our friends," partners, peers, and clients, my wife Patricia and I built frog design into a strategic agency jewel with over 450 employees and nine offices located in cities around the world. The company represents the permanent vanguard in the arena of strategic design and business innovation.

Naturally, any reasonable person may wonder why such major global giants as Disney, Microsoft, General Electric, and Motorola turn to an agency such as frog for advice and solutions when they have all the resources on earth at their disposal. Our long-term colleague Steven Skov-Holt answered this question eloquently many years ago: *"Our clients and client companies come to creative agencies because they need . . . radical solutions that they can't get through their own internal groups [and]. . . because tender, fresh new ideas have trouble surviving the toxicity of most corporate settings."*

But we never take our eyes off of the business goals that have driven our success. We—and our clients—understand that design is an integral part of any successful business strategy, and not an artistic "boutique" profession. A temperamental clutch of self-absorbed artists won't form a solid foundation for a sustainable business model. Business design the "frog way" involves attracting the best people to the table, and then providing the environment and leadership necessary to allow everyone to work better by working together. That idea is the secret to frog's success, and the secret to most strategic professional alliances. It's also the central focus of innovative business leaders who are seeking to establish a foothold in an ever-evolving world economy.

o   strategic creativity and sustainable success

When I started working for Apple in 1982, Steve Jobs' ambitious plan to make Apple into the greatest global consumer technology brand on the planet seemed crazy to some. Computers were just beginning to make inroads into professional offices, and home computers were little more than a dream. But that dream was a reality for Steve. He spoke often and confidently about the "consumer market," and soon everyone in the company shared his strategic vision of the future of computers. In a relatively short time, Steve's vision became the world's reality, and it transformed Apple into the design-driven market leader it is today.

I first met Steve Jobs in 1982. I was visiting California, and I attended a party thrown by one of frog's ex-interns, Jack Hokanson. About thirty designers showed up, and Rob Gemmell—a designer at Apple—was among them. He spoke highly about Steve Jobs, saying he had committed Apple to pursuing technical excellence and world-class design. When Apple initiated a global design search, Rob brought my ideas to Steve's attention. Steve and I met in person (his T-shirt beat mine that day in the "old and worn" competition) and the ball started to roll.

Jerry Manock and Rob narrowed the competition to just two studios—one of which was frog. While our competitor represented a very European design focus, I tried to reposition Apple as a California-global brand—Hollywood and music, a bit of rebellion, and natural sex appeal. frog built about forty models to demonstrate our concepts and we arranged them in a meeting room at Apple's headquarters, creating a virtual showroom of the company's future. When Steve and the board members entered the room, they smiled and said, "Yes, this is it!" frog's radical design language became known as "Snow White" and it provided the born-in-America gene for Apple's DNA. A dramatic departure from the clunky, olive-drab look that dominated computer technologies at that time, our design language evolved from these strategic decisions:

- Apple computers would be small, clean, and white.
- All graphics and typestyles had to express cleanliness and order.
- Final forms would offer smart, high-tech shapes, created with the most advanced tooling.
- All product designs would adhere to an environmentally friendly "No paint—less cost" rule, based on treating ABS plastic and all other materials with care.

Steve Jobs and I also agreed on one guiding principle: "Do it right the first time." Steve offered me a long-term contract on the condition that I move to California and duplicate our Altensteig facility close by Apple. We shook hands, and that handshake launched one of the most decisive collaborations in the history of industrial design. frog's investment in this nine-month competition had cost us more than the $200,000, but we were richly rewarded with an annual retainer ten times that. In return, we made good on our promise to set up shop in the San Francisco Bay area (which, twenty-seven years later, remains the home of frog's headquarters).

Although the Snow White design language was an important part of my work at Apple, my real challenge was to help launch and build the company's true American-Global cultural brand statement. Our goal was to use a young and dynamic design language to change the way the world viewed Apple, its products, and the very act of owning and using computer technology. The Apple IIc was one result of our collaboration, and it was a huge success—over 50,000 units sold during the first week following its release. The Apple IIc was named *Time* magazine's 1984 "Design of the Year," and now rests in the Whitney Museum of Art's permanent collection. Apple's revenues climbed from $700 million in 1982 to $4 billion in 1986.

More importantly, our collaboration set the stage for Apple's design-driven approach to business. Today, no other company in Apple's space has its kind of flawless and disciplined brand, product, and consumer-experience strategy. Steve and his team have infused the Apple brand with design. Every product promotes an identity and a clear idea of the customer experience it provides as part of the bigger Apple "ecosystem." When consumers buy a product that has been "Designed in California," as the Apple label proudly proclaims, they are buying into a way of life. Design has rooted Apple in its own cultural context and extended its influence into the global marketplace.

The global success of Apple's creative strategy—and that of numerous other clients we have had the privilege to work with over the years—illustrates that, contrary to what many business leaders think, the world is not flat. It is a round and roiling tangle of complex cultures, each separated from the others by its unique needs and expectations. We, the people who occupy this corrugated landscape, are defined by our history. Our traditions, politics, and religions inform our lives and influence our decisions—from whom we marry to what we buy. In a flat-world marketplace, one size fits all, but fitting a business to the intricate contours of the real world is a far more challenging prospect. That's what makes design such an important part of any creative business strategy, and it's also what has placed it in the driver's seat of the new creative economy.

Today, the business world is engaged in a global battle between individualism and collectivism or "Culture versus Commodity," as I call it. As companies dive for the lowest costs, they abandon highly qualified local workers and place their bets with low-cost labor overseas—all under the "Flat-World" banner of cost-efficiency. As we've now seen, strategies that boost the bottom line in the short term often result in unsupportable losses down the road. Businesses that sacrifice their unique strengths for the safety of shared efficiency make losers of us all. They rob us of meaningful jobs, even as they diminish the economic and cultural value of once viable and innovative brands.

In fact, the old Flat-World economy couldn't be "won," and now it can't even be defended. Yes, by cutting cost and driving scale, businesses have helped to make high-tech products and digital services like computers and cell phones affordable beyond the most optimistic projections of even ten years ago. But the dirty by-product of these stunning technological advances is a world dominated by products that lack any semblance of human or cultural context. These mass-produced, mass-marketed objects don't provide any type of inspiring consumer experiences. And, in markets divided into high-end luxury and value-driven cheapness, competitive strategy becomes murky. How can a company add true value or even just visually differentiate its low-cost cell phone from those of its competitors, when all of them are designed and manufactured in just five or six Asian factories?

Creative strategy offers clear benefits over the traditional supply-chain-dominated approach to business. It results in human-adaptive solutions and not in commodity-like products for which nobody is willing to pay full price—especially when the offerings outnumber the buyers. Strategies based on creativity, insight, and cultural awareness are more environmentally responsible and sustainable than the age-old approach of winning through maximizing your use of resources, money, and people. It is a cold fact that both manufacturing and service industries are hitting the ceiling of efficiency and scale. Only strategies that explore and take risks—those that are willing to surprise and inspire on a human scale—can hope to win in our evolving economy. Adopting a creative strategy, in other words, boils down to a fundamental and momentous shift in how one thinks about business.

Today, frog design, along with strategists, designers, and their business partners around the world, are faced with a new opportunity, as businesses seek answers to the dwindling prices, profits, and identity offered by markets clogged with "me too," mass-produced consumer products. Creativity is the new major driver and a multi-billion-dollar segment of the new economic order. And design is the means by which companies can apply creativity strategically to their business purpose. Great leaders understand that truth and embrace the power of creativity and innovation as they drive their organizations toward a more prosperous and sustainable future.

2

true lies
the role of leadership
in innovation

"If you see the bandwagon, it's too late."
—JAMES GOLDSMITH

"When your numbers are good, you're good" is a common refrain in the board room, but savvy investors want to know how good your numbers will look in three to five years. Long-term success requires that organizations remain focused on a well-articulated business strategy, and the responsibility for maintaining that strategic focus rests with the organizations' leadership. Without the support and guidance of strong leaders, any larger strategy will stall in its initial stages. Successfully forming and implementing strategic goals is a creative act in and of itself, and it requires leaders who share a fundamental understanding of the role of design in promoting a culture of innovation throughout the business. Although few corporations mirror the smooth operations spelled out in their press releases, the internal discord that results from a lack of shared vision at the leadership level can destroy a company's coordinated pursuit of a design-driven strategy of innovation.

My first lesson in leadership came to me as a twenty-year-old lieuten-ant in the German army. I had joined out of high school, and in less than two years found myself in charge of thirty-five cadets, most of them older than I was. I quickly understood that posing, preening, and pretending wouldn't help gain the respect or cooperation of my troops, and that to be a true leader, I had to be authentic and caring. I've learned a great deal more about leadership since then, of course. In addition to building and running my own business, I've had the good fortune to work with the leaders of some of the most dynamic companies in the world and to observe their successes and failures. I've seen that great leaders have the ability to develop new and better strategies aimed at possibilities that others can't even comprehend. And that kind of foresight comes from a place of creativity.

Creative strategies involve outsized risks that can only be managed through ethical decisions. But idealistic goals and principles alone won't cut it; companies also have to establish specific methods and processes for implementing a creative strategy, and they must be guided by inspired leadership. That's the art of business.

○ seeing the future and supporting bold initiatives

The power of bold and inspired leadership is clear in the story of Apple. To this day, Steve's focus on building Apple into the greatest consumer technology brand in the world hasn't wavered. He has a sometimes-dictatorial manner that irritates a lot of people, but he's also a charismatic leader who inspires a deep-seated trust among his workers. Steve demands a lot from his team, and typical corporate mediocrity is not an option. He is and always has been the sole authority in determining what makes an "insanely great" Apple product and what doesn't. Fortunately, his judgment is almost always right on—and when it isn't, it's close.

Most people underestimate Steve's personal loyalty and integrity. When I worked with him, he didn't agree with every detail of my work but he did defend it against the naïve and politically motivated criticism I received from the majority of his established team (including Paul

Kunkel, who later wrote a largely inaccurate and trashy book about Apple's design in those early years). Steve wasn't the only one at Apple who supported our bold design initiatives. Andy Hertzfeld, Bill Atkinson, Joanna Hofmann, and Susan Kare, among others, were great to work with and showed real understanding and enthusiasm for the new design language Steve and I wanted to introduce throughout the company and its products.

To convert the Apple brand from a Silicon Valley start-up to global player, the company had to change its design and engineering processes as well as its industrial model. Steve recognized the masterful production processes taking hold in Japan and Singapore, and one of the first steps he took toward the "new" Apple was to launch several important collaborations with Asian electronics companies. The Macintosh SE and the Apple IIc were in some ways Samsung-like products, because they were produced in Samsung's Singapore manufacturing plant.

Apple's global relationships didn't end in Asia, nor did its pursuit of design-infused technology. In fact, Apple made an under-recognized breakthrough in the 1980s with its advances in desktop publishing. Our goal was to move beyond the horrible graphics of dot-matrix printers, so Apple began by licensing modern typestyles from the German typesetting company, Berthold. We then took Canon's high-end copy engine and combined it with a Macintosh board, which had the capability to process the high-resolution PostScript graphics of scalable fonts, and added a "soft window" user interface. The printer was an instant success. With it, Apple pioneered an entirely new industry for design software (companies such as Adobe wouldn't have started without it).

Even back in the 1980s, some companies used outsourcing to overseas businesses as a means of cutting costs. But Apple—which at that time had yet to build its strong legacy in R&D and production—was the first American electronics company to intelligently use collaboration and highly integrated outsourcing with overseas partners. To manage these external collaborations, Apple closely guarded its intellectual property. Rather than merely "dumping" its manufacturing processes in a foreign land to capitalize on cheap labor, Apple worked in close collaboration with its outsourcing partners, and it paid them for their original ideas and developments. In other words, Apple learned to form close working partnerships with overseas firms, rather than mortgaging its intellectual capital to boost the bottom line—a strategy it continues to follow today.

Yet, in the midst of this progress, Apple's board ousted Steve Jobs. Although Jobs officially resigned from the board, the founder was essentially forced out of Apple on June 4, 1985; I remember the date well, because Steve and I were spending a lot of time together back then, and my wife and I ended up canceling a party we'd planned for my birthday on June 5. Forget all the so-called rational explanations for this decision: Apple's board was either misguided or just plain stupid. But the repercussions of Steve's dismissal serve as a perfect example of the connection between bold leadership and the sustainability of success.

After Jobs left, Apple CEO John Sculley appointed Jean-Louis Gassée as head of Macintosh design, and the two took sole reign of the company. They quickly built market share and the stock did very well, prompting outside financial analysts and investors to heap lots of praise on Apple's new leadership. In addition to the excitement caused by the initial stock surge, observers raved about the company's creative strategy. But these outsiders failed to grasp that the new team was simply cashing in on the success built by Steve Jobs. Worse, the public had no way of knowing that Apple's leadership was actually spending its innovation "capital" without generating more.

This wasn't a uniquely "Apple" experience. Corporate dysfunction is often masked by the effect of asynchronous timing—the crucial time delay between executive decision, implementation, and results from the marketplace—that can make it very difficult to gauge the effectiveness of current leadership. Even many business leaders fail to grasp the simple fact that the success a company enjoys today is the result of good decisions its leadership made in the past. At even the most successful companies, stock market investors have to trust that the leaders are continuing to generate the good decisions necessary to build their organizations' future success. But outsiders—including financial analysts—never really know what kinds of decisions leadership is generating within an organization at any given time. This was certainly the case with Apple in the wake of Steve Jobs' departure, which occurred shortly after we introduced the "Snow White" design language. Our designers continued to work with the company on an exclusive retainer. The story I saw unfolding inside Apple was very different from the one being fed to the public.

At every level in the company, Jobs loyalists were replaced with what I judged to be rather mediocre talent. Eventually, I myself was forced out by a dull, ruthless engineering manager I found to be clueless about design and culture. Rather than guiding the engine of Apple's innovation, Sculley and Gassée's mission seemed focused on changing everything Steve Jobs had valued, by moving the organization from the cutting edge to the middle of the road. That decision was a train wreck in the making—and a huge waste of creative potential.

Then, Apple's poor decisions began to play out in the marketplace. In the early 1990s, Sculley, who had assumed the role of Apple's chief technologist, pushed the incompletely developed Newton handheld computer to market. In spite of the bizarre level of hype surrounding its release, the device was too slow, tried to do too much with too little, and failed miserably at fulfilling Apple's gold standard of usability. The company's product strategy faltered, too, as it became diluted and patchy. Many designers merely peddled their personal tastes under the Apple brand, and, apparently, no one inside the organization had the good judgment to realize that the company's products had become boring and ugly. Ultimately, it would take another ten years—and a return to Steve Jobs' leadership—before Apple could turn its fortunes around.

With Apple's profits stalled, John Sculley left the company in 1993, after the board had installed Michael Spindler as Apple's new CEO. Michael is a very fine man, but Apple was a sinking ship with too many holes for one man to fix. After he left in 1996, Dr. Gil Amelio took over as CEO, a decision that was about as smart as "having the boars doing the gardening" (a German proverb that might be tough, but in this case, dead on). After Amelio uprooted and tossed aside one-third of the company's employees, and after Apple's stock dropped to a twelve-year low, Apple's board accepted his resignation and brought back Steve in 1997.

By then, Microsoft, Compaq, and Dell had redefined personal computing. Sony, Panasonic, Phillips, and Samsung were asleep at the wheel, lacking the drive (or ability) to converge hardware with software and content. When Steve was back in as iCEO (interim CEO) he asked me for strategic input and I recommended that Apple become a new kind of consumer-experience-driven company. (I also recommended that he make peace with Microsoft.)

As always, Steve listened. In the years since his return he has focused on converting Apple from a computer company into a provider of digital consumer experiences. He's had great success in revitalizing the organization—he even made peace with Microsoft (well, partial peace, anyway). Steve has had one success that should be of special interest to business executives and designers—Apple's savvy strategic use of outsourcing the "right" way. The company partners and communicates well with original design manufacturers, while co-designing and working closely with its own manufacturing and development teams to ensure its products offer exactly the right kind of user experience.

Apple also pays the original design manufacturers (ODMs) for designing to its specifications. By faithfully executing Apple's product definition, ODMs such as Foxconn and Inventec have built their prime-market presence by being the willing executor of the Apple product definition. These kinds of partnerships aren't difficult to manage, but they do require that companies spend a great deal of time with their ODM partners, building trust and getting the relationship right. This kind of investment has paid off handsomely for Apple, as it can for other companies that have the benefit of bold, visionary leadership.

○ building a culture of innovation

As Steve's story illustrates, strong leadership is essential for cultivating a corporate culture of innovation and strategic creativity, and the savviest leaders build such a culture by fostering strong relationships with creative professionals both inside and outside the organization. As I noted earlier, that kind of leadership represents the art of business. For many creative people, however, the business world has nothing to do with art, and that's unfortunate—for them. Designers become masters of their own fate when they master the workings of business and learn to appreciate the rational thinking, vision, ethics, and creativity it takes to run a successful organization. Designers become true professionals (albeit sometimes rebellious ones) when they grasp the connections among business, money, and power, and then use their creative competence to arrive at the same goal their business partners are working toward.

Successful designers are collaborators. Their tools and media are human and social entities like companies and industries, and they often work with groups of people in the converging fields of science, culture, and economics. They create products and experiences for mass consumption, and their work must have both emotional and rational power. Designers couple artistic talent and creativity with sound understanding of business structures, processes, goals, and alliances. They draw upon all of that background knowledge to convert technology and market knowledge into emotionally compelling products and experiences that profit both consumers and businesses. At least that's how it's supposed to work.

Without strong leadership to support those goals, however, designers can find themselves caught in a battle of cultural and philosophical differences with their business colleagues. Some call it a left-brain–right-brain disconnect, but it's about more substantial issues than that. Challenges go well beyond the give-and-take of human personalities and egos. Design-driven innovations don't succeed as often as they should, and many failures occur because designers don't carry the same clout as their business clients and bosses. Creating sustainable success for business is difficult, and the process comes with a variety of obstacles for designers, executives, and the organizations they serve. Business executives often are hamstrung by a host of issues within the company, and they simply can't train people to have a single-minded focus on new product development. Radical new directions raise well-founded and substantial worries about costs, pricing, profits, and losses. And many executives work within fractured corporate structures made up of walled-off business units and divisions. The pressure to avoid risk and limit exposure to internal criticism in such a segregated and disunited organization places rigid limits on corporate decision-makers.

In the end, business and economics are essentially human adventures. They may strive for rational objectives, but the driving elements behind them are most often irrational and illogical. Outsized egos, personal ambition, defensive behaviors, and inaction all can wreak their own damage on the innovation process. The bigger the company, the more likely it becomes that executives, managers—even owners—will fall for the temptations of internal competition over the goal of winning in the marketplace. When this happens, petty politics, intrigues, and personal rivalries erupt—very much to the disadvantage of the company and its employees, shareholders, and customers. It takes nimble leadership and keen strategic vision to guide organizations safely through these rocky waters.

I've had ample exposure to leadership's struggle on the path toward innovation. Design careers are formed, after all, through work at those earliest developmental stages of innovation, where decision-making processes and inner-office mechanisms are truly tested. To illustrate how leadership succeeds—and fails—at the innovation process, let me share with you some of my observations and experiences from the front lines of the business/design partnership.

○ maintaining strategic focus and creative capital

Apple's struggle to maintain its strategic focus offers an excellent example of the challenges companies face in dealing with evolving leadership, economies, and marketplaces. But Apple isn't the only big-brand company to have exhausted its creative capital while riding on past successes. Consider Motorola's handling of its mobile phone brand. When Ed Zander took over as CEO in 2004, the late brand visionary Geoffrey Frost had already repositioned Motorola's brand with his "Hello, MOTO" campaign, which included the Motorola RAZR, a radical new redesign of the company's cellular phones. The RAZR was a great departure from Motorola's previously bland products, and its sexy new design made it an instant success—in spite of its clunky software.

Many acknowledged that the RAZR's software was difficult to use, but no one at Motorola fully recognized the negative impact of the software's interface on the user experience. The company and its analysts even praised the decision to sell Motorola's stake in Symbian, the wireless operating system company in Cambridge, England, to Nokia. Instead of advancing the RAZR strategy by improving its user-interface software and creating new products for 3G and easier pocket computing, Motorola's managers and engineers "stuck to their knitting." The company tried to capitalize on its past success by producing a series of phones with tweaked exterior designs—the SLIVR, ROKR, PEBL, and KRZR—but none of them did as well as the RAZR.

In January of 2005, frog approached Ron Garriques, then executive vice president in charge of Motorola's cell phone division, with a different proposal. I tried to convince Ron that to really capitalize on RAZR's success, the company needed to pursue a more user-friendly product strategy by making all major software features directly accessible with a maximum of two "clicks." Initially, Ron was interested but, as our proposal went through Motorola's internal "bottom line" vetting mechanism, the company decided that launching the new user-interface software program would require the efforts of three hundred people over two years, at a cost of $50 million. In other words, there was no chance that our idea was going to fly.

After our proposal was jettisoned, Ron's strategy was to "buy" market share with low prices, while also positioning Motorola as the mobile phone industry's leading hardware performer—even though the new product designs for the SLIVR and other Motorola phones were under-performing with the same crippling user interface. When the RAZR's product life ran out after about two years, so did the company's strategy, and Motorola's stock value began to drop. The losses in both money and market share kept mounting, until Motorola's wireless business went up for sale in 2006. Ron went to Dell the following year. As the marketplace shifted toward smart-phone devices such as Apple's iPhone, even Motorola's traditional competitors Nokia and Samsung began taking away its market share, and the company found itself struggling to stay alive in a market it had helped to create. The fall was fast and hard, offering ample proof of how quickly a company can lose its strategic focus when leadership blinks.

○ promoting ethical innovation

It's easy to recognize the mistakes a company makes after the failures have played themselves out, but I still wonder why business executives aren't willing to overcome executive egos, internal politics, and a lack of foresight before things come crashing down. A myopic view of the bottom line may have something to do with it. As we've seen during the dot.com boom and bust of the 1990s and the economic crash of 2008, speculation and paper wealth can lure plenty of smart people away from their better judgment—and into a morass of compromised ethics.

The importance of ethical leadership in business cannot be overstated. Being ethical isn't just the right thing to do, it's also a matter of self-interest. Businesses that compromise ethics drive away many investors and consumers, who feel they can no longer trust the leadership's decisions. And many talented people are hesitant to join a business with a reputation for unethical practices. In short, failures in ethics mortgage a company's future. Studies show that, when ethical lapses go unpunished, they become standard operating procedure within the offending company or organization. Most players in business make an honest effort to be ethical, but it's a fight to stay that way because of intense competition in today's marketplace. Business leaders who fail to think through the ethical implications of their decisions, strategies, and business model put their companies at a great and unnecessary risk. That's why a strong commitment to ethical practices is a fundamental responsibility of leadership and a core element of any organization's creative strategy.

Making the right decisions for shareholders and investors is important, but leaders must also recognize that meeting their responsibilities to the community—the employees, families, and local economies surrounding their company—is just as vital to their lasting success. Not long ago I was involved with Maytag, the appliance manufacturer formerly based in Newton, Iowa, and I saw firsthand what can happen when a company ignores this responsibility.

Maytag has long been one of America's most recognizable brands. Its hugely successful and long-running advertising campaign featuring the lovable under-worked Maytag Repairman earned the company a place in American hearts. In the 1960s, its brand popularity stood shoulder-to-shoulder with that of Coca-Cola and McDonald's. Unfortunately, the consumers' goodwill couldn't shelter Maytag from the seismic changes taking place in the appliance market—changes that the company's leadership refused to acknowledge.

When companies achieve the level of trust and brand recognition that Maytag built over the years, their incredible competitive advantage gives them unique opportunities for innovation. Those were opportunities Maytag desperately needed during the late 1990s, when the company's sales began to flag.

Sometime around 1998, we got a call from Maytag, asking us to prepare a pitch for creating a new website for the company. Naturally, I knew the brand and its reputation as an organization "In Search of Excellence." As I learned more about the company, however, I saw a much more complex picture. Over the years, Maytag had grown through acquisitions and addressed vertical markets by traditional pricing-pyramid tactics. It carried a broad collection of product lines, such as Jenn-Air, KitchenAid, Magic Chef, Amana, and Hoover, resulting in strategic brand chaos. Maytag's products and those of its sub-brands were out of synch with new trends, such as appliances for smaller families and single households, and it had stumbled in its attempts to implement innovative features such as stain-based washing processes. In spite of these shortcomings, many of the company's brands were in high-price market segments, where success pivoted on innovation and cutting-edge design. The company's strongest advantage lay in its workforce. Its production workers and engineers were highly skilled and took great pride in the quality of their products. But Maytag's executive management was tightly focused on the "corporation," rather than on products and the quality of the user experience they offered customers.

Clearly, Maytag needed much more than a new website. We at frog proposed a platform project, which would bring advanced digital user features to a pilot product across their brands. Maytag's development teams reacted positively, but warned us that it might be difficult to win

management support. Our efforts had stalled for months, when something good happened: Lloyd Ward became the new CEO, and after some
strong inside lobbying, he agreed to see us. Ward had experience with
both Procter & Gamble and PepsiCo, and he clearly understood marketing strategy and market shifts. He showed some initial interest in our
proposal for a new product development model, in which all departments would collaborate and communicate openly throughout every
stage of the development process. The model we proposed required a
commitment to develop trust and positive synergy between departments,
as well as a change of the broader corporate culture.

Sadly, we failed to convince Maytag's leaders. Whether it was Lloyd
Ward's reluctance to impose such sweeping changes or the resistance of
executives defending their turf, we couldn't get Maytag to implement this
strategic shift. Our engagement with Maytag felt like a defeat for me, but
in years to come, Maytag faced an even greater loss. Instead of building
on its brand loyalty by placing innovative and inspiring products as the
keystone of the company's sustainable success, Maytag chose to cut costs
by laying off thousands of workers and outsourcing manufacturing
to Asia. The move was a betrayal to Maytag's entire community—its
employees, the town of Newton, its customers, and its industry. Thousands of people lost their livelihoods for a move that did nothing to solve
the company's fundamental problem—the need for improved products.

Had Maytag developed a creative strategy to address this problem,
it could have redefined itself and its industry by manufacturing ecologically friendly, energy-efficient home appliances. The country's relative
affluence and growing interest in environmentally responsible living in
the late 1990s could have helped Maytag's products perform better than
those offered by low-cost competitors. Perhaps more importantly, the
company could have provided a positive and inspiring experience for its
customers, who were mostly hard-working American families with children. This kind of ethical industry leadership is at the very heart of innovation and design-driven strategy.

In the end the Maytag's board decided to sell the company to Whirl-
pool, who essentially took on the company's brand and retail "shelf

space," but not its people or factories. The design center and factory in Newton was closed for good in 2006, leaving the community of Newton, Iowa, in tatters and sparking an outcry among local politicians, who defended their constituents by demonizing the practice of outsourcing. But outsourcing wasn't Maytag's biggest misstep. Instead, the company's downfall can be traced back to the lack of vision on the part of its executives. Had the company's leadership avoided those spectacular failures by making a strategic effort to rejuvenate the Maytag brand, they could have kept Maytag in play as a viable, American company—one that embraced its ethical responsibility for the future of its workers and customers.

◦ sustaining success

In 1982 Tom Peters and Robert Waterman wrote *In Search of Excellence,* in which Maytag featured prominently as a shining example of business excellence. Despite what we know now about Maytag's subsequent downfall, Peters and Waterman's principles of success are as relevant today as they were then. Those principles are founded in American-Puritan values of hard and honest work, respect for the individual, love for doing business, and appreciation for the values upon which any democratic country is built.

Change is constant, and companies need to be in a position to lead that change—or at least prepared to get off the wave they're riding before it breaks. *Excellence* offers ample proof that no single, unchanging strategy can carry a company forever. The "excellent companies" Peters and Waterman profiled in their book include Bechtel, Boeing, Caterpillar Tractor, Dana, Delta Airlines, Digital Equipment, Emerson Electric, Fluor, Hewlett-Packard, IBM, Johnson & Johnson, McDonald's, Procter & Gamble, 3M, Amdahl, Atari, Avon, Bristol Meyers, Data General, Disney Productions, Dow Chemical, DuPont, Frito Lay, K-Mart, Levi Strauss, Mars, Maytag, Merck, Wal-Mart, Texas Instruments, and Wang Labs. Most of these companies have gone through some sort of crisis since 1982, and some of them, such as Atari, didn't make it through. IBM and Delta are among those that recovered from disaster, but only as distinctly different companies. It's also interesting to note the companies that failed to make Peters and Waterman's list, including General Motors, General Electric, Lockheed, and Xerox. These are significant businesses today, but each of them ran into some kind of fundamental trouble in the years prior to 1982.

Clearly, leaders can't allow their companies to rest on their laurels. Without periodically tweaking its strategy, no business, no matter how successful it seems, is going to remain competitive in the long run. A truly excellent company is continually planting seeds for future harvests. That sounds easy enough, but it's a big challenge for leadership. Investors want to see immediate returns in the stock market, and they generally look unfavorably on funneling company resources into research and development—even though those investments are the lifeblood of sustainable success.

This odd market dynamic breeds company introversion and complacency. Without consistent external rewards for innovation and growth, businesses that are successful and growing lapse into internal competition, department to department, even team to team. They start to miss trends and changes happening outside the traditional domestic and global consumer dynamics. And, inevitably, those lapses in foresight eventually demand that the company rivet its focus on avoiding failure, rather than on achieving success.

When true leaders leave because of age, death, or firing, the organizations they led to glory must quickly find another special person to take the helm in order to avoid faltering. Sony is a good example of how businesses can stumble when passing the torch to next-generation leadership. The remarkable ascent of that company is well known, and I am personally very proud to have been a part of it. But the company today is very different than it was when Masaru Ibuka started "Tokyo Tsushin Kenkyujo" (Totsuken) or "Tokyo Telecommunications Research Institute" in 1945, then partnered with Akio Morita to found the company we are all familiar with today. What most people don't realize is that when Ibuka San and Morita San left their operational roles, grew old, and eventually died, Sony lost more than just its founders. It lost its soul.

At its zenith Sony was a radical and idealistic innovator that delivered complex high-tech solutions with products that appealed not only to consumers' ears and eyes but also to their minds and hearts. After Masaru and Morita left in 1994, Norio Ohga—my personal mentor—was the logical heir to the Sony throne. Ohga San worked very hard to fill his predecessors' shoes, but he simply couldn't rally Sony's various divisions and their egotistical leaders into one strategic effort. Then, in the late 1990s, when Ohga chose Nobuyuki Idei as his successor, the house of Sony truly began to crumble.

I met Idei San in 1974, when he was Norio Ohga's assistant. I quickly recognized that he was a brilliant manager and a quick learner with a sharp, at times cynical, wit. Even so, as CEO he just didn't have the Sony leadership "touch." Idei San's problem as a leader was not so much that he was inexperienced or overwhelmed with the diverse demands of Sony's business. More importantly, he didn't recognize new, outside opportunities for convergence and he lacked the tools and the personality to convert or fire the dissenters within his organization (and there were quite a few who needed to go). More than ever before, Sony needed a grand and simple vision, one that articulated a convergent strategy and issued a rallying cry throughout the many diverse departments within the company. Had Idei San been able to pull that off he would have become a true hero. Unfortunately, he couldn't.

As a result Sony split into multiple business divisions—almost like fiefdoms—that cared more for their own survival and success than for the success of Sony. Sure, the company produced great new lines of products, such as the digital Walkman, PlayStation, and VAIO computers. But there was no core vision for the Sony brand, and there was no strategic convergence of the company's hardware, software, and media content. Even the Sony Style retail shop strategy became a half-hearted affair.

All of these problems stemmed from Idei San's inability to unite Sony's new middle managers in pursuing Sony's core value, "simple is best" (and "best" in Japanese also means "most difficult to achieve"). For all their bravado, those new managers were ignorant of the realities of leading a business on the global scale that Sony and the digital consumer electronics industry had assumed. As a result, they drove the company into a wall. In Idei San's last year as CEO, Funai, a lesser-known Japanese ODM that, among other things, supplies electronic products to retailers such as Wal-Mart, outperformed Sony by a margin of four to one on profits. Sir Howard Stringer succeeded Idei San as CEO in 2005. At the end of his first year, profits were down and overall results were mixed, and the company saw further lackluster performance in 2008. No matter how many people love Sony—I still do—most would admit that the company has not maintained its position as one of the world's most innovative brands. In fact, it may actually be headed for even deeper mediocrity unless Sir Howard can push the company back to Sony's core values of strategic unity and simplicity.

Of course, new leadership doesn't have to bring with it the kinds of problems experienced at Sony. I witnessed a very different "changing of the guard" in my work with Henri Racamier, former CEO of Louis Vuitton. Henri was a retired steel magnate and a millionaire who took over operations of Louis Vuitton at the request of his wife, Odile, the granddaughter of company founder Georges Vuitton. From 1977 to 1987, Henri transformed the company into one of the world's largest and most profitable luxury goods groups. Henri achieved that success by carrying on the company's core value of producing high-quality, luxury products, while updating its approach to exclusivity by making those products available to a wider consumer market.

When I started to work with Henri and his team in 1977, Louis Vuitton had just two shops—one in Paris on the Avenue Marceau and one in Nice—that generated about $14 million a year. By then, Louis Vuitton bags and suitcases already had reached cult status with fashion-savvy customers—especially those from Japan. Lines commonly extended into the street outside the Louis Vuitton store in Paris, and the company maintained a two-bag-per-sale limit to prevent customers from reselling the luggage elsewhere. Henri, however, was not content with selling bags and suitcases—his vision for the company was much larger than that. He set about transforming the Louis Vuitton brand into a totally new type of luxury goods experience. And he did it without sacrificing the traditional values of the company's founder.

Part of the transformation of the Louis Vuitton brand involved a new design principle, developed through Racamier's collaboration with frog design—a strategy we referred to as "non-matching." Traditionally, women matched their handbags to the style and color of their clothing, which meant that they needed a lot of different handbags. We discovered that Vuitton's original brown-golden "Etoile" and "Chess" patterns—designed to hide scratches on luggage—were considered "neutral" in regard to changing seasonal fashions. We extended this idea of "neutral" design to colors, and created a line of leather handbags and luggage cases designed to be standalone products, with a classic look that could transcend the seasons and, indeed, the years—a line of Vuitton products that would appeal to women and men, regardless of their social status and age.

The appeal of "LV" became so universal that everyone from ladies in high society to movie stars to prostitutes the world over began to carry Louis Vuitton bags with pride. The new branding wasn't designed specifically to appeal to a global audience, and it didn't downplay the company's French roots. Louis Vuitton remains a Parisian brand (thus the words *"Malletier a Paris,"* or "luggage maker to Paris," on its labels), and its French cachet has helped the brand manage to keep its cult status. However, today, you see the LV brand on high-end products around the world (and you don't have to wait in line in Paris to buy a bag).

As this new branding took off and the company started to grow, Henri pushed for top partners in marketing and communications. One of his most brilliant and audacious moves was to turn the qualifying races of the America's Cup into the Louis Vuitton Cup. Then, when Vuitton revenues reached about $700 million in the mid-1980s, Henri recognized that the company's value put it in a potentially vulnerable position as a target for acquisition. To defend his company against a hostile takeover, Racamier merged Vuitton with Moet Hennessy, creating a company known as LVMH.

Ironically, the success of the LVMH merger ultimately cost Henri his position. Henri left after Bernard Arnault mastered a successful takeover of LVMH in 1990—yet another example of a capable successor taking over the leadership role of a successful company. In another irony, however, Arnault's takeover helped to keep Henri's legacy alive. Arnault expanded Henri's successful "affordable luxury" strategy by adding a cluster of luxury consumer brands—such as Fendi, TAG Heuer, Kenzo—to the LV stable, and in so doing, continued to build the company's success.

After leaving the company, Henri ran Orcofi, the consolidated company that oversaw the Vuitton family assets, and he continued in his role as a passionate and important benefactor to the arts, especially music. Henri never lost his energy and excitement for life. He died in 2003 at the age of ninety, while doing what he loved most—traveling in Sardinia. In his obituary, *The New York Times* noted that, when he left LVMH, the company had 130 stores around the world and revenues of $1.2 billion. In the third quarter of 2008, the company reported double-digit growth in a struggling marketplace.

o o o

Each of the successful leaders described in this chapter had both a grand vision and the unique ability to bring that vision to reality. That said, success is not only a product of inspiration, big dreams, and a charismatic personality—although those must certainly play a role. The best leaders and the most successful companies also have the will and the desire to explore the unknown. And they have a deep and ongoing respect for design and its power to drive a strategy of creativity and innovation.

After forty years, when I think back to the leaders who have inspired, taught, and supported me, including those I describe in these pages, I'm still most grateful for the guidance and leadership of my earliest mentors, who inspired me and taught me to exercise my talents through hard work. Yes, the years have proven to me that many businesses are driven by a relentless search for better "numbers," rather than a visionary pursuit of innovation. But I've also seen that those companies can't achieve the long-term sustainable success that results from creative strategy and design-driven excellence. That kind of success requires strong leadership, defined by its strategic vision, its ethical commitment to serve people and society, its courage to pioneer new pathways, and its ability to turn dreams into reality.

3

designing to win
the creative business strategy

"Take time to deliberate, but when the time for action has arrived,
stop thinking and go in."
—NAPOLEON BONAPARTE

As the great coach Vince Lombardi said, "Winning is an attitude—unfortunately so is losing." In much of the business world, the fear of losing greatly overshadows the desire to win. Driven by that fear, most companies strive to conform to the standards of rational, measurable, and cheap, in effect, seeking success through mediocrity. Real life, however, doesn't work that way. The majority of challenges that confront business decision-makers—whether inside their companies or within their consumer market—turn out to require emotional, ambiguous, and expensive solutions. That means there's a gap between corporate business strategy and how the rest of the world really works.

To close that gap, business leaders and executives turn to consultants like frog to help take them to the next stage of strategic development. We've seen how design-driven innovation can establish a creative foothold for businesses, and how strong, foresighted leadership guides the way toward sustainable success. But when it comes to taking the first step down that path—building a winning business strategy and a tactical plan for its implementation—businesses need the collaborative firepower of creative minds. As strategic creative directors, the best design firms know that devising an early stage or "pre-PLM" (product lifecycle management) business strategy is vital for successful innovation. It cuts to the chase by revealing the realities of both the marketplace and the company's capabilities.

Some of the most valuable lessons and advice I've gathered in my professional career have come from Japan and the Japanese. Kenichi Ohmae's classic book, *The Mind of the Strategist,* has been an especially invaluable source of information on business strategy, and I think it's as relevant today as it was thirty years ago. One of Ohmae's key recommendations is a great example of the ongoing Japanese theme I mentioned in the previous chapter, "Simple is best." "*In the construction of any business strategy,*" he writes, "*three main players must be taken into account: the corporation itself, the customer, and the competition.*" Pretty straightforward advice, but (again) not so easy to follow.

Common wisdom holds that business people are well organized and rather conservative, whereas creative people are more chaotic and progressive. For Kenichi Ohmae, however, creativity and organization aren't mutually exclusive, nor are conservative business practices and progressive ideas. In fact, he suggests that some elements of the creative approach are crucial to establishing any winning business strategy: "*The true strategic thinker can respond flexibly to the inevitable changes in the situation that confronts the company,*" he writes. "*And it is that flexibility which, in turn, increases the chances of success.*" Ohmae also tells his readers that strategy is both a rational and an emotional sequence of steps and that the best way to approach it is to dissect complex challenges into solvable tasks. Ohmae is talking about both strategy—the long-term planning of actions in order to achieve a certain goal or to win against competitors—and tactics—the actions one takes to implement strategic decisions. And in this chapter, we're going to take a closer look at how business leaders and designers collaborate in constructing and implementing winning creative strategies.

○ the strategic plan

The flexibility of creative strategy is an essential part of the culture of design. Change is the designer's mantra. In fact, at frog we once coined a slogan—"Change Is Fun"—to acknowledge this cultural principle and remind us of our responsibilities to adhere to it. It also reminds us as designers to reach forward to new possibilities and to never lose sight of the satisfaction of strategic success and the victory our clients can achieve with a unique competitive advantage. After all, winning is what business is all about. As the military strategist Shun Tzu observed, it is victory, and not mere perseverance, that is the essential goal of any battle.

Successful business strategy reveals its most critical military roots in its reliance on planning for the use of future resources (new technologies and trends), and the response to future threats (such as global warming). Business strategy plots the long-term direction of a company or a brand. It has to target the right kind of market, one whose needs best match the company's specific competence. And sound business strategy has to account for the company's available resources, as well as those that must be acquired or developed in order to outperform its competitors in this market.

This kind of success can only be achieved in collaborations where all partners understand the fundamental role of creativity in the strategic plan. Business leaders who view design as little more than an aesthetic "fix" for dull and naïve business models might temporarily look good in the media, but their moments in the spotlight are brief. It takes a day to make a fascinating "study," but years to create a new strategic business. Let's take a look at some of the common elements of the most successful creative strategies.

The Fourth Line: Building Strategic Reserves

The great Roman strategist, Caesar, understood that, even under the most stressful situations, an army still needs reserves. His famous "fourth-line" strategy of calling up fresh, hidden forces in the heat of battle earned him yet another chapter in the history of strategic warfare. This same level of foresight and long-term preparation is necessary for any strategy meant to outlast immediate, short-term obstacles—whether an onslaught from a stiff competitor or a lack of consumer spending due to a faltering economy. Smart leaders have to plan for holding the line of market share and profits, but at the same time they won't win without strategic reserves—new business concepts or some dormant potential they can leverage to counterattack and gain market share on their own terms.

The rebirth of Apple can serve as a good example of this strategy in action. By the late 1990s, the company was buckling under increasing pressure by Dell, HP, and other personal computer brands. Apple's Macintosh market share was in the low single digits. The company looked like a goner. Industry analysts declared that Apple had to begin competing in the personal computing market or become irrelevant. That's when Steve Jobs came back in as CEO.

The first tactic Jobs used to implement his plan to regain Apple's stature in the marketplace was to stop the market share bleeding by launching new products with flamboyant design and a new operating system. As far as his competitors knew, he was betting on the only strength Apple had left at the time: design and usability. But these long-time hallmarks of Apple's products weren't the only weapons the company could muster. What Jobs' competitors didn't see—and what he set to work developing—were the company's creative resources in digital convergence. When Apple began introducing products that offered holistic customer experiences based on the synergy of software, hardware, and the Internet, Dell, HP, and other PC brands were outflanked. Their strategies didn't prepare them to compete on Apple's new playing field—they didn't own the right software or they couldn't adapt their product lines to these new uses. So while his competitors were focused on defending their success in the personal computing market, Steve Jobs opened up a whole new line of attack by creating new and uncharted markets. The first result of this strategy was the iPod/iTunes line of products. The second was the iPhone.

This hidden "fourth line," a reserve of new product development and innovation, caught Apple's competitors off guard and precipitated a rash of chaotic reactions on their part. When HP's then-CEO Carly Fiorina tried to play catch-up with her "digital consumer strategy," she made a deal with Apple to sell its iPod under the HP brand—but without any design change. Naturally, consumers saw little reason to buy what appeared to be an Apple product from HP. When Fiorina finally pulled the plug on this naïve venture, it was too late for HP to get into this new and booming market with a product of its own. Dell stayed closer to its comfort zone and simply put its logo onto an otherwise generic music player, but that strategy didn't work either. Dell's player looked boring, whereas the iPod (leveraging Apple's initial strengths) offered a fresh, exciting design.

In the meantime, Apple's disruption in the marketplace allowed it to regain relevance as a mind-share leader. The company followed its new momentum and began to make headway in the personal computing sector with dramatic gains for its Macintosh products. Apple's coup de grace was the launch of its own retail stores, which set a new retail-experience standard of excellence in shop design and customer service and created a cultural and inspirational context in which Apple products could shine even more brightly.

Beyond its classic use of the "fourth-line" approach to overwhelming the competition, Steve Jobs' reinvention of the Apple brand demonstrated two very important truths about strategy: First, a good creative strategy can define which external—and uncontrollable—factors might influence a company's potential opportunities. Second, winning strategies are based on the values and expectations of those who have ownership and power in and around the business.

Achieving Measurable Success Through Relative Market Share

The goal of any business strategy is to achieve measurable success. The business world constantly produces metrics and spreadsheets by which to judge its success, but analyses that narrowly focus on profits can't tell the full story of competitive strength. A company's relative market share—its market share divided by that of its strongest competitor—is a better indicator of success, because it reveals how successful the business is in relation to its greatest threat in the marketplace.

Remember, only the market leader has a relative market share larger than 1. For example, in 2006, HP had a global market share in PCs of 17.4 percent with Dell, their closest competitor, at 13.9 percent. If you do the math, that means HP had a relative market share of 1.25—which isn't that much.

HP's printer division is a different story. The company had a global market share of 49 percent in 2005, with Samsung as their closest competitor at 8.7 percent. This means HP had a dominant relative market share of 5.6. Even more staggering was Apple's May 2008 grip on the digital music player market, with its iPod Media Players at about 71 percent and its nearest competitor, San Disk, at 11 percent. That mean Apple's relative market share for the iPod was 6.5.

To build a broader position in the marketplace, HP's leadership needed a plan to improve its standing in the PC market. By the same principle, Dell needed to get into the printer business, which it has done. Apple's iPhone is a strategic keystone for the company, because the company's leaders understand that any smart phone with media player capability is going to command a bigger and bigger percentage of the digital music player market.

So far we've been talking about relative market share and how it applies to large, global players in consumer technology (companies, it should be noted, that depend almost entirely on outsourcing partnerships with ODMs in Asia). Let's now have a look at a group of small and midsize industries, where the metrics of relative market share offer a far more valuable indicator of success.

The German Mittelstand companies (*Mittelstand* translates to "midsize") of the early to mid-20th century offer fine examples of small- to medium-sized companies that became the true engines of an economy. These enterprises were largely owned and controlled by single families who defined a relatively narrow niche market and became experts in serving that market.

Today, Mittelstand companies remain a big part of the German economy, and many economists refer to them as "hidden champions." For these companies, relative market share not only separates leaders from followers, but is also a much more valuable indicator of success because the businesses still use a fully integrated supply and value chain (the complex processes of moving a product or service from the suppliers to the consumer and the manufacturing steps that add to the products' final value to consumers). Also, unlike the big global players, Mittelstand companies own and control their own intellectual property, both in innovation and processes.

In 1996, leading Mittelstand companies in Germany (such as Trump, a global leader in laser cutting and metal shaping), held a relative market share of 1.56. Today, in response to economic pressure in the form of competition from Asia and new investments in green technology, the Mittelstand advantage has grown to about 2.3, which means that the Mittelstand leader's market share is 130 percent larger than that of its larger competitors.

The secret to this success lies in strategy and the Mittelstand owners' passion for improvement and innovation. These competent company executives worked hard to become leaders in a difficult and very specialized market—a market that's big enough to grow to a couple of billion dollars with staggering profit margins, but too small for the "global giants" like Siemens, GE, or Matsushita.

The Mittelstand companies also benefit from their strategic locations. Most are based near mid-size or large German cities with very good universities, so the companies have both a local supply system for equipment and materials and a pool of highly skilled crafts people and qualified employees. The communities created around these companies are tightly knit, as most employees also share social lives, through soccer clubs and other cultural and social gatherings. This social organization introduces a valuable ethical element to the mix, tied directly to the concept of community that we talked about in Chapter 2. When everyone in the company knows each other well, they have greater respect both for co-workers and the company. Before a great product is commoditized and outsourced to low-cost labor in another country, people in successful mid-size companies come together to innovate a better solution. In the process, they quite often achieve the impossible, and at a price much lower than that of a wholesale layoff and relocation.

○ the tactics of creative business strategy

A smart, creative strategy will position a business well, but even the best strategies succeed only if they're implemented with well-chosen tactics. Innovation can be a key tactic in business, especially when it leverages existing resources rather than new technologies to fulfill customer preferences. In its development of the iPod and iTunes, for example, Apple's winning innovation tactic was to integrate, refine, and compress existing technologies into a seamless, convergent customer experience. Taking a page from Kenichi Ohmae's playbook, Apple's innovation was a simple solution that required a complex blend of visionary leadership and a committed corporate "community."

The story of the Mittelstand success in relative market share also reveals parallels between the tactics of creative business and military strategies. Caesar knew that smaller units were more capable than large armies, because they could communicate more efficiently and respond more readily to the unexpected. Caesar also mentored his troops and promoted from within, while encouraging an open-minded and honest exchange of strategic intelligence. The German Mittelstand companies seem to have studied their ancient Roman history. They, too, mentor and promote from within, and they have a collaborative corporate culture of open communication that helps everyone in the organization form a realistic view of the competition and the market, rather than swallowing the sugar-coated, feel-good appraisals often fed to company executives. These strengths promote a culture of innovation and collaboration that is an essential tactic for capturing relative market share in a fiercely competitive market.

I've seen this collaborative culture in action—sometimes, even extreme action. Once, frog was hired to design a very innovative product for a German company, and the owner-CEO invited about twenty people to attend the first briefing, so we could get a clear understanding of the company. Of the people in the meeting, only four or five were "suits." The others worked on the floor, in production, logistics, quality control—even a cafeteria worker was brought in, because she "knew everybody in the company." I also learned that some of those attending the meeting were retirees who lived near the factory. In assembling this group, the owners' logic was simple: Everyone in the room was deeply connected to the company and because of that they were able to speak out confidently. If there were other ideas or resources in the company that could help us, they would know what they were and they would tell us—and they did. The owner-CEO also understood that, even though "creativity" may be an elitist process, it can't simply be injected into a small, self-confident company. To succeed, creative strategy has to be based on a common cultural understanding.

Winning requires the creative management of people, visionary leadership to put together a process, and the bravery and loyalty of the entire organization to see it through. In the end, victory is about knowledge and opportunity. Successful business strategists see opportunity at hand and marshal creativity to devise the tactics necessary to ensure victory—by winning the marketplace.

○ the evolution of successful strategy

Naturally, as the leader of frog, I had to practice the same lessons of strategy and tactics inside my own company, while teaching them to our clients. When I found a strategy and process that worked well, we used it for all it was worth. But at the same time, we were aware that no single strategy works forever, especially in the realm of technology and design. My goal was to remain ahead of the curve by years. I pushed my own team to continually analyze and adapt our strategy and tactics, and we ask our clients to do the same. And frog's approach to business—along with its approach to creative strategy—evolved dramatically over the past forty years. Let's take a look at some of the unchanging principles that have helped guide that evolution.

Only the Best

As you read in Chapter 1, in 1968 and 1969, I started out with some objectives, which are as relevant today as they were back then. These principles continue to define how we at frog do business (see the sidebar, The Four frog Principles). Ultimately, all these objectives were compressed into one slogan, which I had learned and admired as an engineering intern at Mercedes Benz: *ONLY THE BEST.* That slogan means many things—only the best work, only the best clients, only the best strategies, and only the best implementation. When you want to be the best, you can't be dogmatic—you have to work to win. When something works well, you try to get better at it; when something goes wrong you learn from it, and move on.

I put all these ideas to use back in 1972 when I landed one of frog's first big contracts with KaVo (Kaltenbach + Voigt, now owned by Danaher/USA), a privately held dental company that had industrialized the dental air turbine. When I first met the head of research and development, Martin Saupe, he showed me around the company's engineering departments and its very impressive factory. I noticed right away that KaVo's R&D group wasn't coming up with the kind of products the factory was capable of. I immediately thought, "Here's a tactical opportunity." I'd been asked to design a new light for one of their existing chairs, but I realized that we could and should imagine something bigger. As it turned out, the project became a life-changing venture for both KaVo and frog.

I knew going into the project that only the best work would do. My partners Andreas and Georg and I had just one week to prepare for the pitch meeting and, for the next seven days, the three of us worked day and night to conceptualize an entirely new dental system. The design had better ergonomics than anything on the market as well as a more advanced focus on hygienic materials and state-of-the-art production specs. We made 1:1 scale models of the key components like the treatment chair. We also built a 1:10 scale model of the whole system, made with a perfect finish so we could get nice photographs for our presentation. The last night before the pitch, I went to bed at 1 o'clock in the morning. Four hours later, after they had developed the films, framed the slides, and wrapped the models, Andreas and George woke me up. By the time I was ready to go to the meeting, they were already asleep in the studio.

When I showed our models and explained the new system to Martin Saupe, he was blown away. I was certain that our hard work had paid off.

the four frog principles

About forty years ago, I scribbled down these four objectives and they remain a valuable guide to frog's continuing goals:

1. *Find your "sweet spot."*
   To establish the best arena in which to compete, I looked for the one area in design where I was very good and where others were not—and that was the field of electronic technology design. Due to my studies in engineering, I knew the thinking and processes of electronic technology better than other designers, and I understood the complexities of its design, production, and support. (I also respected collaborative processes and the financial balance among investments, cost, and returns.) This arena was very attractive to me, because I was both ambitious and rebellious and I wanted the pleasure of shaking up the establishment, beating them with better work.

2. *Be business minded and do great work for clients—and for your own company.*
   This sounds like a simple idea, but it is one of the most difficult challenges for many in design. At frog, one major component of following this principle was to work according to our client's economic needs. Another big challenge was to promote our work in the most professional ways—including building a strong brand. I think that frog was the first design agency to run a global advertising campaign in specialty magazines.

3. *Look for "hungry" clients who want to get to the top.*
   Everything depends on partnering with great clients. At frog, I focused on ambitious, global companies with huge upside potential in technology who were or wanted to become the best in the world—and had the financial ambition and means to do it.
   We at frog had great successes following this principle with companies such as Sony, Apple, Microsoft, and SAP.

4. *Get famous—by being the best.*
   I had to use this principle as a goal—otherwise I would never have achieved it. I wanted to be world-famous at age thirty-five, and was lucky enough to do so. But in the process, I learned that I had to be appropriately grateful to all who helped me gain this success, and I had to continually justify my fame through good and hard work. All of us at frog remember and follow the lessons we learned in applying this principle to our work.

But there was one problem—and it was a big one. After complimenting me on the quality of my pitch, Martin asked me to come look inside a cabinet in his office. In it, I saw about twenty small-scale models from other design companies, mouldering on the shelves like headstones in a creative cemetery. Martin Saupe obviously didn't understand the radical departure our proposal had taken, and he told me he needed "more time to think about it," which meant that he was going to pass on our project.

"Nothing but the best," I thought. Scrambling to save the pitch and not let our week's worth of work go to waste, I asked Martin Saupe to let me speak with the final decision-maker at KaVo. After a little back and forth, Saupe agreed to call the owner and CEO Kurt Kaltenbach and his CFO, who were in a meeting just one floor above us. I could tell that they were reluctant to meet with me, but Martin—perhaps inspired by my persistence—made a good sales pitch, and up we went to the next level of "command."

I set up my projector as soon as I got to the meeting room, but kept the models under wraps in my box. Then I proceeded to explain how the system we were proposing would shift the company's strategy, position-ing KaVo not just as a company selling dental systems, but as a company selling holistic treatment solutions that provide a healthier work environ-ment for the dentist and make going to the dentist more bearable for patients. As I spoke, I projected the images of our new system, called Estetica, on the screen—and they looked great. But I kept the focus of the pitch aimed squarely at describing the new strategy KaVo could embrace in tandem with the new product (you learn more about our work with KaVo and the role of envisioning future strategic goals in the innovation process in Chapter 4).

At the end of the presentation, Kurt Kaltenbach said, "This is what I have been waiting for all my life!" We signed a contract on the spot, and the relationship with frog lasted for more than three decades, until Danaher/USA bought KaVo in 2003.

Getting the KaVo contract was a great victory for frog, but as you can see, victory would not have been possible if I hadn't stuck to frog's stra-tegic goals and "only the best" principle, by pushing for a much more radical and better solution than KaVo originally asked for, and by persuasively arguing for a chance to present my ideas to the organization's top-level decision-makers. In fact, adhering rigidly to strong principles and a passionate desire to win with integrity actually makes it easy to be flexible and pragmatic in the pursuit of success, because you never have to question the reasons driving your efforts.

Of course, over the years and with other clients, frog has constantly refined its strategies and adapted its tactical solutions. I've learned, for example, that quick and easy acceptance can sometimes be a bad sign for a creative project. Anything really new has to be able to overcome violent emotional opposition—and that's a long process, requiring more understanding and commitment than you might need to trigger a snap decision. And because not all of my clients are like me, frog built an agency of personalities, which provides its clients with many good choices for forming a creative and collaborative partnership. Still, all of these personalities are guided by a single strategic vision, rooted in principles that have helped frog attract only the best people, clients and employees, alike.

Adapt to Win

At frog, we try to learn and experiment on a constant basis. My wife and partner Patricia and I call this strategy "Outside-In"—the idea that we succeed by creating what our clients really need most, rather than by simply trying to replicate our own past successes. Change is the only constant in the company (positive change, we hope), and that means that frog is a "moving target" for its competitors. We know that we have to be able to adapt in order to win.

Because it is poised to adapt, frog lives happily on the borderline between art and commerce. For all those who struggle with conflicting notions of how design can live in a business model, here's a magic formula that might help resolve the conflict—a formula that after forty years remains one of frog's key strategic assets:

$$CULTURE + PROCESS = PROFITS!$$

A deep knowledge of and appreciation for cultural values is essential to forming any creative strategy, but so is an understanding of process. Process-oriented and human-minded collaboration is scalable, and it enables organizations to remain nimble and ready to adapt to new developments, demands, and opportunities, so that organizations can grow and explore new areas without a loss in quality or financial performance. Process orientation also enables companies to define—and achieve—goals. Of course, this type of adaptive strategy leaves no space for ego-maniacs, cynics, or prima-donnas, a beneficial "limitation" that keeps even the most creative consultants connected to the mundane realities of daily business life.

When I started frog as an industrial designer in 1969, my focus was on creating well-designed technology. That was a relatively new idea at that time, and I was able to develop it solely because of my personal motivation and my education. In 1974, when I started to work with Sony—at that time, the best consumer-technology company on earth—converting extreme technology performance into globally acceptable and admired branding statements ("It's a Sony") was my paramount concern. In other words, design became a means to achieving a higher goal for my client.

In 1975, I applied what I had learned at Sony to my own company, by starting frog on a path away from pure industrial design. As a matter of fact, if frog had remained rooted solely in industrial design, we would have ended up as a "design boutique"—an arena that works fine for so-called design stars, but not for business designers who need scalability. We would have been limited in our ability to constantly explore new opportunities—in other words, to "follow the money." This same notion of adaptation allowed frog to change again in 1982, when we won Apple as a client and were able to bring to that relationship the skills we had learned at Sony in outsourcing and co-development with partners in Asia (you learn more about this experience in Chapter 4).

That move positioned frog for yet more successful collaboration. When we saw the ascent of analog-digital convergence, we extended our design processes into the digital domain. During the mid-1990s, frog was a pioneer in user-interface design. We worked with Microsoft on the development of Windows XP, with SAP on R/3 and Web Weaver, with Sprint-Nextel on its wireless user interface, with Qualcomm's development of the BREW platform, and with a host of other tech companies that needed to turn their programming-driven software mazes into efficient and enjoyable user experiences. Since 1998, we've been mastering outsourced product lifecycle management (PLM) and supply chain management (SCM) processes.

After learning the hard way through some near-misses with its own product ventures (which I describe in the next section of this chapter), frog was able to create some very convincing and highly profitable successes with Disney's consumer electronics division. In that venture, we went directly to the "big-box" retailers, such as Target, Best Buy, and Circuit City, to find out what types of Disney-branded products they wanted to carry. Working with Disney, the retailers, and the ODMs, we then designed specific products with an authentic Disney look and feel. By cutting out the "middle man," we were able to offer the products at low prices, yet maintain healthy profit margins. And we didn't have to spend our time and money selling our products to retailers—after all, we'd created exactly what they'd asked for. Over a three-year partnership with Disney, we helped design and deliver a range of successful Disney consumer electronic products, such as the Disney PC, TV, DVD player, and the Mickey Karaoke Microphone System with built-in songs. From exterior hardware designs to digital user interfaces, these products consistently captured the essence of the Disney brand.

frog's relationship with Disney actually started back in the mid-1990s, when we assisted Disney in evolving the implementation of its own business strategy, through the redesign of the Disney cruise ship line. Back then, Disney wanted to extend the length of family visits to its resorts, and so it needed a cruise ship designed to appeal to family members of all ages. When we first met, Mike Reininger, then Disney's vice president for product development, asked me to think "less about maritime architecture and more about package design." We went to work with great support of John Heminway, who was a "universal consultant," and set out to recreate a classic ocean liner—back then a virtually extinct species—as envisioned by parents and their children. We analyzed the look of the historic Normandy, a French cruise ship with elegant proportions and a sloping stern. Then we projected ourselves into the future, looking at the designs of the fictional Star Trek *Enterprise* and cutting-edge futuristic aircraft. We conducted studies of people of all ages, and we talked to the professionals—officers and sailors who wanted a "real ship." We matched classic maritime colors to Disney's own black-red-gold-and-white theme, and we designed a gem-like bridge. When our studies revealed that kids wanted more than one funnel (which is all that's technically necessary for the ship), we added a purely decorative front funnel with a café on top that offers a fantastic view.

When everything came together, our design encapsulated an amazing blend of historic elegance and futuristic fun—and it met Mike Reininger's early-stage strategic objectives. To describe the *Disney Magic*—our first ship, which was followed a couple of months later by the nearly identical *Disney Wonder*—I coined the term "retro-futuristic," a look that went on to influence global design in a wide range of products, from automobiles to electronics and fashion.

As it develops new strategic-creative relationships, frog never stops adapting. Recognizing the advantages and challenges of ever-earlier decision making, frog developed a strategic consulting practice in 2004, through which we enabled our clients to test and visualize a number of product strategies using reality simulations. And, in 2005, with the backing of our new parent company, Flextronics, Inc. (an international contract manufacturer that purchased a majority interest in frog in 2004), frog became even more competent in the vertical integration of convergence products that combine software and hardware, especially in the medical field.

Today, frog has found a new "sweet spot" between the proven high-level business consulting services offered by major firms, such as McKinsey or BCG, and the more traditional practice of "design by briefing," that still represents the lion's share of most major design agencies' business. frog's clients understand the value of this new offering very well, as our growth in revenues proves.

I call frog's niche "frog space," because it truly operates in its own. Our adaptability and our deep understanding of process and culture enable us to offer creative-strategic solutions within multiple paradigms such as design, engineering, consulting, or innovation. And, although change is the only constant for frog, we haven't abandoned the design and consulting space. In fact, it serves as the foundation for the work we're doing in the development of pre-PLM hardware and software. We are able to help clients at a fraction of real R&D investments by providing strategic advice and testing our discoveries against realistic scenarios that include technology, competition, social and cultural behaviors, and sustainability.

The internal challenge for frog in its ongoing process of strategic adaptability is the same as that for other innovation-led businesses: to manage the chasm between the more abstract excitement of business strategy and the designers' sensual passion for individuality and originality. As businesses adapt to meet new market needs and opportunities, strategy must lead, design must contribute. Ideally, innovative companies attract and mentor hybrid talents who can do both. Realistically though, the solution for successful adaptation lies solidly in building teamwork and cultivating both the "right" and "left" brains of the business.

Learn from the Things That Don't Work

I can honestly say that frog's incredible post-2001 success in the development of software, physical products, and digitally defined customer experiences would not have been possible had we not suffered what many considered to be an abject failure. At frog, we pride ourselves on constantly learning, constantly adapting, constantly expanding the limits of what we've previously believed to be possible. But no business that embraces innovation as a defining force can escape the occasional misstep. Fortunately, we sometimes learn the most important lessons—and grasp the most important opportunities—when we stumble.

By the end of the 1990s, the demand for frog's intellectual capital was high. Over the preceding decades, we had formed incredibly successful collaborative partnerships with some of the world's leading innovation companies, including Apple, Sony, and Samsung. As our successes gathered public attention, other companies sought to mirror our approach to the innovation process. During our collaboration with SAP in 1999, Howard Lau, then the director of SAP's venture fund, asked if we could scale any of frog's process knowledge into a software application. In effect, he was asking if we could shrink-wrap frog design into a software program.

The idea was appealing. The dot.com bubble was still expanding and venture capitalists were throwing money around like freshly fallen snow, especially in the area of "creative collaboration." When we considered that, with a collaborative commercial enterprise software product, frog could spin off a standalone Internet software company, we decided to give it a shot. At the time, however, frog was a global leader in user-interface design but had little expertise in programming capabilities. To bring those skills to our development process, we acquired the programming boutique agency Gravity in San Francisco. We also launched a new research and development team in Herzliya, Israel.

In effect, we were coordinating a variety of very different teams across an entire company—a process that should have played on frog's strength as a collaborative partner. For years, we at frog had been telling our clients that, in order to succeed, an organization needs to consider all of its relationships—both inside and outside the company—as long-term, collaboration-based experiences. Often, however, collaboration and communication between our own teams was strained at best. At other times, it was non-existent. And then we discovered that some companies involved in our project were outsourcing development to remote partners and vendors. We had to address these issues frequently in order to keep the project on-track.

In the meantime, we had begun working toward the major goals for our software product. One of the key challenges in any company is promoting open collaboration with honest and timely communication. To make the development process more efficient and collaborative (both within and between departments), we decided to include in our program a digital database "warehouse," where various departments within an organization could easily store and access ideas and process models. Over time this data would become a collective corporate "memory," or even better, a "creative corporate mind." We called our new product "bizwerk."

In bizwerk, we developed "smart documents" that could connect vital data across various internal departments within a company. For example, if a product marketing team needed finances to develop a product, the bizwerk software could automatically initiate the request for that funding by updating relevant documents within the financial department's record base. At the same time, bizwerk would help the financial department begin forecasting and planning for associated costs in engineering and other departments within the organization that would become involved with the project over time.

Normally, this kind of information is kept secret within a company, but, when any department safeguards its information from the rest of the company, political infighting can break out and slow the entire organization's efficiency and competitiveness. Having experienced this kind of non-productive quagmire, the CEOS, CFOs, and divisional VPs of the companies where we workshopped the bizwerk concept loved our idea. They wanted to use bizwerk as a tool for transparency and better results in the marketplace. Even engineers and marketers had positive responses to our software, after we did a couple of dry runs with them.

Eventually, however, we would hit a wall of resistance, and in most cases it came in the form of a company's IT department. Traditionally, IT buyers are rewarded for avoiding disaster, not enabling success. They look for tools that can be used by lots of people with average talent, not sophisticated products that enable a few talented people within the company to do even better work. In that environment, IT buyers are rewarded for avoiding disaster, not enabling success. bizwerk was too risky for them. As I've said before, risk avoidance often trumps an organization's desire to succeed.

After a series of unsuccessful pitches to U.S. companies, we looked to SAP, the company that first inspired us to develop our collaboration software. In early 2001, I flew to SAP's German headquarters with four key members of our bizwerk team for a "strategic alliance session." The meeting started out amicably enough—but it didn't end that way.

First, SAP's team members showed us some collaboration software they'd been using, and we saw right away that they needed something new. Their current set-up was a sort-of thin-client website/technical worksheet hybrid, with an email component thrown in. Not only was the software nearly irrelevant for any design processes the company would need to pursue, but it really didn't support any other essential business function either. It was absolutely awful.

After we demonstrated bizwerk to them, SAP's team was extremely excited. After four days of working with SAP, we had a contract that had been negotiated down to the last detail of our product's design, features, and capabilities. Everyone was ready to sign—everyone, that is, except Achim Heimann, the head of SAP's PLM group. At the last minute, Heimann suddenly dismissed bizwerk as impractical and unworkable. He criticized multiple aspects of our product, including its information architecture, "fat client," and more. With our contract in the trash, we headed home from Germany, confused and frustrated by our abrupt dismissal by SAP.

While we could only speculate on the reasons behind SAP's sudden change of course, it marked the end of frog's bizwerk venture. We had run out of gas and, after an investment of about $6 million, we were out of money too. To save frog, we had to pull the plug, deal with our frustration, and dig our way out of a financial crisis.

But in the end, bizwerk wasn't a failure at all. In fact, the lessons frog learned on that particular journey launched us on the road toward our most lasting success. By diving so deeply into the inner workings and processes of business, we saw first-hand the antagonistic relationship between strategic creativity and tactical supply chain management. More importantly, we discovered how to make that relationship far more productive. As a result, frog landed in a unique position. We knew how to combine the early-stage innovation and product-development process (including the exchange of early-stage concepts and ideas) with any global, multi-billion-dollar production system. At that time, frog held the corner on that expertise—no one else in business consulting or manufacturing came close to our level of knowledge in this area.

frog's subsequent success in the development of software, physical products, and digitally defined customer experiences would not have been possible if we hadn't had the bizwerk experience. And, although we understand that brand ownership and control is vital, we now believe that to use the frog brand to create our own "products" would have limited or even killed our consulting business. In short, bizwerk was an economic failure that gave birth to frog's ultimate competitive advantage, and a perfect example of the invaluable lessons to be learned from things that just don't work.

○ designing the ultimate strategy— with the right creative partner

Not all designers share the same goals, nor should they. Part of my goal with this book, for example, is to show how design can be combined with strategic goals and tactical implementation to create a much more potent and relevant tool for business. That said, design can exist without strategy. In fact, the strength of the link between design and strategy is directly related to the school of design in question. To fully appreciate the potential impact of design on business strategy, it's important to understand the four schools of design—and types of designers—an organization might be working with.

The first school is represented by "classic designers," such as my friends Dieter Rams and Kenji Ekuan, the late Ettore Sottsass, Jr., Mario Bellini, and Jonathan Ives. These designers can run their own studios or be corporate stars. Ten or fifteen years ago, I would have included myself in this group. This school's approach to design is both logical and visceral. In other words, designers in this school generate individualistic-artistic statements that balance an appeal to the heart with an appeal to the mind. This school of design addresses the bigger goal of making products more usable, enjoyable, and safe.

The second school of design is represented by "artistic designers" who rely on visceral methods to create products with spectacular visual appeal. This group includes designers such as Philippe Starck, Karim Rashid, and Ross Lovegrove—a man who, many years ago, was frog employee number 18, and who remains a good friend of mine. (He still is thankful that I encouraged him to design what we jokingly referred to as his "Italian shit.") The work of these designers draws the attention of a significant portion of the popular media (consider, for example, the

Style section of *The New York Times*), but it often isn't suitable for sizable organizations interested in scalability. Artistic designs can be difficult to replicate and apply. The work of artistic designers often isn't easily replicated and can rarely be applied in industries with complex challenges of usability, technology, and logistics (for example, software or consumer tech). Nevertheless, these designers inspire the world on a broad scale and their work offers a prototypical approach that others can use to create derivative products requiring lower levels of technical complexity.

The third school is made up of those who work in anonymity in corporate design departments—and includes the majority of designers working today. Some companies use their internal design teams very effectively. Olivetti set a great example about forty-five years ago, when it arranged the collaboration of internal designers such as Hans von Klier with outside consultants, including Mario Bellini and Ettore Sottsass. The results were stunning and resulted in products that inspire us to this very day. But, more often, corporate design departments fall prey to a lack of strategy and identity within the company. The story is sadly common: Internal designers often are mismanaged and underappreciated. They work in organizations that have no consistent approach to incorporating design into their strategic plans or processes, and they report to marketing or engineering managers who have a minimal understanding of the potential of design.

Microsoft's Zune music player project is a good example of what can happen when business managers are put in charge of a strategic design process that they fail to understand. We all know Microsoft is a global leader as a software company, but it has far less process and business experience when it comes to convergent hardware. From a business standpoint, the company could have created a powerful new strategy with the Zune. Microsoft could have hired a strategic-creative consultancy like frog, with competency in vertical hardware and software supply chains, to work with its internal designers in creating a unique new product—a success that could have been on par with that of Apple's iPod. Instead, the company's managers chose to hire Toshiba to manufacture the Zune hardware, resulting in a visually modified Toshiba product with limited online capabilities. The Zune has zero "Microsoft DNA" and by all accounts has had middling success. And remember, Microsoft is a company with $40 billion in cash and a 90 percent market share with Windows/Vista. There's really no excuse for the company's decision to shortchange the development of this potentially important product line.

And this brings us to the fourth school of design, which is made up of highly creative, strategic designers who are fluent in convergent technologies, social and ecological needs, and business. That's the school of design we have been developing at frog today, and the one I'm hoping all of my students at the University of Applied Arts in Vienna, Austria, will represent when they enter the workforce. Our mission as holistic designers—and the mission that all business leaders should adopt for their organizations' design efforts—is to create physical and virtual objects that are inspirational in their usefulness, beauty, and social/environmental responsibility, while at the same time supporting the business's strategic goals. This mission forms the foundation for any organization's creative strategy and drives its tactical implementation. For business leaders pursuing an innovation-driven business model, strategic designers are essential partners.

Lao Tzu described the essence of strategy when he wrote that *"one who does not compete, cannot be competed against."* I take this to mean that we can impose crippling limitations on our own goals when we compete only against outside forces. Instead, we must constantly try to surpass our own best efforts, and we should look to ourselves for the key to that strategic success—important advice for both partners in the business/design collaboration. As designers, we are uniquely qualified to feel and see opportunities that might be invisible to our more "rational" professional partners. And the business leaders we partner with may be attuned to exciting opportunities that haven't even crossed our minds. In the end, creative strategists in both business and design must grow to the task of working together to build a brighter future for themselves, their organizations, and their world. That is the ultimate strategy for success.

4

minds beat money
the innovation process, step by step

"If I'd asked people what they wanted, they would have said 'faster horses.'"
—Henry Ford

"Innovation" has been a buzz word in the business community for quite some time. Unfortunately, a lot of people who talk about innovation don't really understand what it means—a fate it shares with the term "design." That's a pity, too, because innovation and design are two of the most powerful forces for crafting a more successful future for almost any business. But, to use these tools to their fullest potential, you have to know what they truly represent.

Although commonly equated with the creation and implementation of new products and processes, innovation, which comes from the Latin "innovatio" (to create something new), takes many forms. Through the process of innovation, an engineer may strive for technical improvements, a designer may create a human-driven usability advantage or a new experience, and an executive may develop a new business model.

Innovation isn't about getting lucky or finding cheap shortcuts. It's about transforming business and building potential. Innovation companies typically share certain characteristics. They tend to be financially lean and fit and—most importantly—their leaders are curious and tenacious. These leaders understand that innovation is much more than "new ideas" and that, without the meaningful context of a strong innovation process, ideas aren't worth anything. And, as we learn in this chapter, while setting, ideation, and implementation are important elements in the innovation process, so are the innovators themselves—the actual people working in the field, their executives and managers in the larger organization, and their creative collaborators.

From an economical perspective, innovation is a matter of life and death. A company must innovate today if it wants to be in business tomorrow. For a company to succeed, it not only must be much better than any of its competitors, but it also must anticipate where its future competition will come from, and what it will offer. Today, business leaders are turning innovation into a major driver for better solutions, experiences, and sustainable business. In fact, the most successful leaders apply innovation across every business process, from behavioral strategy and market research to financials, leadership, and business models.

Carrying off that kind of cultural revolution within a corporation can be a tall order. In *Leading the Revolution*, Gary Hamel describes the reluctance to change as a key challenge for business leaders trying to infuse their organizations with innovation: "*. . .despite all the pro-innovation rhetoric that one encounters in annual reports and CEO speeches, most still hold the view that innovation is a rather dangerous diversion from the real work of wringing the last ounce of efficiency out of core business processes. . . . As change becomes ever less predictable, companies will pay an ever-escalating price for their lopsided love of incrementalism.*"

Innovation isn't just the after-glow of a flash of insight. To create meaningful innovation, we have to inspire, mentor, and shepherd new ideas, and we have to be willing to pay the price of bold, up-front shifts that will help us avoid that "ever-escalating price" of incrementalism Hamel warns of.

So how does a company become an engine of innovation? Although humans and the organizations they create are all unique and unpredictable in their strengths and shortcomings, most successful innovators follow some common steps in the innovation process. Here they are, in a broad and simple outline:

Step 1—Groundwork: Preparation and research require **competence**—knowing the business's goals and design's role in achieving them, and taking both very seriously—and **selectivity**—choosing the right teams, partners, clients, and projects.

Step 2—Creative Collaboration: Successful, results-driven teamwork involves **rituals** such as brainstorming or ideation workshops (such as the frogTHINK process, which I describe later in this chapter) that produce new ideas and opportunities; **projection**, in which all parties in the process envision how the innovation would change the company, the consumer, and the world; and **management**, that promotes group consensus and provides a plan for supporting and shepherding the innovation toward implementation.

Step 3—Marketing: Launching any product, both internally and externally, involves **refining and proving** the benefits of the innovation to the organization, **optimizing** the innovation's role in the business model, and **providing the leadership tools** necessary to take the innovation to market.

Over the years, this innovative process has served me well. Let me show you how it works.

○ step 1: groundwork

Successful innovation builds on effective groundwork. Businesses and those who consult with them need to have a clear and thorough understanding of the organization, its goals, and its challenges. Partners in the collaborative process need to be carefully chosen to leverage the company's (and each other's) strengths and to compensate for weaknesses. And everyone on the team needs to operate from a position of shared understanding, priorities, and mutual respect. The challenges involved in accomplishing this step are significant, but so are the potential rewards for doing it right.

Knowing the Business and Targeting Its Goals

In the face of often brutal global competition, many in business become willing to compromise their company's originality and authenticity. They lose focus on their organization's unique strengths, competencies, and limitations, and in so doing, lose any chance of successfully creating and launching a market innovation. Companies that don't innovate don't succeed. The purpose of any business is to gain and sustain a strategic competitive advantage. To fulfill that purpose, a company has to provide something special—something nobody else is offering in the market-place. Truly great innovations are transformational—both for the inno-vating company and for its consumers—and they spring from the intersecting drives and motivations of business leaders and their creative consultants.

Apple is today's "poster child" of innovation, and many companies want to mimic its success. Broken down to its basics, Apple's path is relatively clear-cut, for those who really want to follow it: Be ethical in your vision, create meaningful and complete experiences for your cus-tomers, use technology for human benefit (rather than for its own sake), and insist on high-quality results.

But adopting the principles that line this path can be a big challenge for organizations with an addiction to "due process" and a penchant for political infighting. That's why so few companies have matched Apple's design-driven success. Those that do—companies such as Toyota, Honda, Boeing, Disney, Nintendo, Genentech, and Docomo—have visionary but realistic strategies and great leadership teams that are changing today's business landscape.

The strongest lesson from Apple and other innovation leaders is not so much about what they deliver in their specific areas of business, but how they managed to develop their innovation-led and defined business model—in other words, how they became an "innovation company." Originally a personal computer company, Apple understood early on that the traditional marketplace of "professional computing opportunities" was crowded with strong competitors such as Microsoft, Oracle, SAP, and Adobe in software and by HP, Dell, and others in hardware. Surveying that competitive landscape, Apple saw little chance for a big win. So the company explored new playing fields by developing its understanding of human of dreams and expectation, as well as by realistically assessing its competencies in hardware, software, and content.

It also chose its partners wisely. In hardware, Apple recognized and took advantage of the value of brilliant ODMs (original design manufacturers) such as Foxconn and Inventec. In software, Apple guided the way in user interface and real-life consumer applications. And it formed groundbreaking partnerships with media companies such as Warner Music and other content owners.

To Apple's advantage, the field of consumer electronics and entertainment was in a sorry state in the mid-1990s. Sony had lost its way, and other big companies like Samsung, Philips, and Panasonic were equally adrift. As start-ups such as Rio pioneered new MP3 technologies (a standard invented by German research institute Frauenhofer), Sony and Samsung saw in them only another hardware opportunity. These companies quickly came up with MP3 players that had very cool designs, but offered dismal user experiences. Uploading digital music to those players was a real pain.

Apple's design team had a more strategic mindset. It saw a huge business opportunity in the design of a better complete music experience. Apple set about creating that experience, and in doing so it redefined and extended its playing field into digital consumer electronics and entertainment. Today, Apple's success in that field is unparalleled.

As we've seen, leadership is required to put innovation to work. Hands-on engagement by top management, corporate alliances, and collaborative processes are vital. Hermann Simon, chairman of the consulting firm Simon-Kucher & Partners and a columnist in Germany's *Manager* magazine, emphasizes in his book *The Hidden Champions* that great leadership achieves its goals by focusing on technology and customer benefit, as well as on finance and markets. "*Ultimately,*" he adds, "*innovation is a mind and process game. Money alone doesn't do the trick.*"

Simon also outlines the economic benefits of top-level leadership engagement in the innovation process. He found that innovation companies—those with a top-down focus on creative, design-driven strategies—typically pay much *less* than many other major German corporations for much *better* R&D.

For the designer, working successfully with major corporations requires some smart and honest networking, resulting in alliances that extend well beyond the business unit or division one is working with. It's also essential that designers do their homework to fully understand the business model, its goals for the innovation process, and its financial capabilities, limitations, and expectations. When everyone engaged in the process grasps and pursues the strategic interests and intentions of the "higher-ups," the innovation team develops a single-minded focus that generates great upward momentum—even as it helps the careers of everyone involved.

Pulling Together the Right Team

As much as any new business opportunity starts with a "brand"—"Just imagine, XYZ wants to work with us!"—successful design collaborations require great business partners—clients who understand that they need help and are ready to share the responsibility of implementing innovation. The human factor in fostering innovation is much more important than many people assume.

Remember: Mind beats money. Good people are more important than good ideas. When you want to create new business success through innovation, you need to work with a team, a partner, or a client who has great untapped potential and who is willing to take the sometimes unorthodox steps required to grow. For creative consulting groups, the best bet is to team up with a client on its way up, one that is just missing that magical ingredient brilliant designers bring to the game: inspired courage fueled by visceral creativity. Such are the majority of frog's clients.

Businesses hungry for a "comeback" also make great collaborative partners. They might have lost out to a new upstart or faltered under the bad management of an "apparatchik," and really want to get back into the lead. With the current state of the economy, these businesses make up a growing segment of the client base for many creative consultancies. Underdogs can find themselves in a good position for innovation, with a renewed motivation and a willingness to take creative risks. Personally, I feel as much satisfaction in being part of major turnaround as I do at helping a new venture achieve lift-off.

In truth, not everybody can (or wants to) be creative. Unfortunately, some of those least capable of understanding the creative process feel compelled to orchestrate it. In the short term, corporate structure can mask an individual's or group's incompetence, but time (and bottom lines) eventually reveal the organization's strongest assets. Businesses are wise to keep those who do not value or cannot recognize creativity out of the collaborative process, and designers should steer clear of partnering with them, although, sometimes, that's easier said than done.

Once, frog was invited by a major U.S. pharmaceutical corporation to deliver a pitch to redesign the container for one of its painkillers. We sat through a "happy-go-lucky, enjoy your popcorn" innovation-kabuki and briefing that left me feeling desperately in need of one of the company's painkillers. The requests for solutions were so overly detailed that they left no space for any substantial strategic thought. The company also announced that it would "rank and measure" our pitch, using a checklist that would have made a Prussian Army logistician proud. Still, we analyzed the company's goals for the project, conceptualized some strategies, and created some initial concepts. I delivered my pitch to a team of what seemed to be very nice people, but their rigid preconditions, misconceptions, and apprehensions made the meeting as painfully awkward as a bad blind date (they solemnly noted, for example, our failure to submit both a red *and* a blue copy of one image). We lost the pitch and, five years later, the pharmaceutical company still hasn't upgraded its painkiller packaging.

This example not only demonstrates the ineffectiveness of the classic advertising agency-style "pitch approach," but also the importance of choosing the right people to engage in the collaborative process. Consultants like frog have the big advantage of always living in the innovation cycle, whereas most of our clients experience innovation only sporadically, which sometimes turns them into kids in the candy store. The art of the process is to balance emotional excitement with professional discipline, and leaders in both design and business are wise to master this art.

Ideally, the collaborative team should include representatives of all relevant areas of the client's business (remember that cafeteria operator in the German Mittelstand company I mentioned earlier?). I also like to have top management involved to the point that the CEO or division leader always knows what is going on, along with strong representatives from marketing, engineering, finance, and factory (supply chain). The team should include some highly critical members, but there's no room for people whose main interests are protecting their turf and promoting their own careers.

Naturally, the client controls the budget, and therefore has the power to staff the team. And, too often, team-staffing decisions revolve around politics rather than expertise or other qualifications. In those cases, something has to give—and I usually speak up, even at the risk of breaking up the project. An honest resignation in the early stages is better than a late-stage failure.

○ step 2: showtime! the creative collaboration

This step in the process is where 99 percent of books on innovation start, and its activities represent what most people think of as the "innovation process." That's understandable. New ideas, in general, are sexy and fun, and so people enjoy talking and reading about the process of coming up with them. In my view, however, the creative collaboration itself is just one of three equally important phases of the innovation process. New ideas are mandatory to innovation, but they're only as effective as the objectives used filter to them and the processes used to develop them.

Ritual: Sourcing New Ideas and Opportunities

The concept of ideation or "brainstorming" originated in advertising. As its use spread to nearly every industry and marketing sector, the practice has become both misunderstood and abused. A cynic once described brainstorming as "two hundred monkeys hitting a keyboard in the hope that they will create a Shakespearean play," but brainstorming can deliver major benefits when it's planned and conducted in the right settings. The first important step in this process is to separate existing thinking patterns and logical arguments from visceral intuition. The second is to focus on the creative process itself—people trusting themselves to think—and not on results. That focus allows participants to enjoy the process without any fear of retribution.

Every company or team possesses huge potential for generating ideas, whether motivated by negative criticism or a positive desire for change. Many of my own personal achievements were based on what I learned by listening to my clients and observing their body language— even when the two forms of expression contradicted each other. Quite often, true leads came to me through secondary conversations, rather than from "vision statements" and official briefings. I'm a big believer in the Japanese notion that we don't "have" ideas, but that ideas "come to us." This non-possessive way of viewing the ideation process is much more effective than the still way-too-popular notions of "my idea" and "your idea." Ideas are agnostic—it's what one does with them that matters.

One of the most successful principles used in the innovation process is to switch ideas—and design concepts—between team members. All too often people fall in love with "their" ideas and, like anyone in love, they refuse to acknowledge its shortcomings and embedded mistakes. And it's important that participants bear in mind another Japanese concept—that people don't "make" mistakes—to say that is to indicate that someone intentionally did something he or she knew was wrong. Instead, the Japanese believe that mistakes simply develop over time. That seemingly simple construct has some important implications. Believing that mistakes simply "happen" avoids blame-laying, and it also opens the door for improving, rather than abandoning, imperfect ideas. By taking a positive approach, this mindset allows innovators to take advantage of acquired knowledge in the pursuit of constant improvement—a pursuit known to the Japanese as *Kaizen*.

Most ideas don't make it through to realization, so the ritual phase gains value from unexpected abilities and rare talents. It also requires some careful attention to the process of ideation itself. Based on our long and global experience at frog, we defined an ideation process we call frogTHINK that has served us well in every collaborative setting. The basic concept of frogTHINK is to collect all available facts and knowledge about an object or experience (including its historic development), and then to "deconstruct" all of that information into its essential elements. The essential element that drives a beverage bottle design, for example, is not functionality or aesthetics but "thirst." To get people into an innovative (rather than rote) mindset, I like to use a practical exercise that involves smashing an inexpensive teapot into bits, and then asking the group to create another object by super-gluing the shards into new shapes (trying to rebuild the original teapot is definitely *not* a creative act). The point of this exercise is important: Most new ideas already exist in the present manifestation of an object, so the challenge is to find them.

The creative collaboration starts with an open mind on a defined stage. The players on that stage are much like those in the ancient art form of Greek tragedy, which remains timeless in its simplicity and its very stringent rules. The action on the stage is created and defined by three elements: the hero (or "leader" in modern business terms), the supporting cast (the organization or company), and the messenger (the irritation or "problem" the innovation is intended to resolve).

Bringing the right players together in an environment that is carefully controlled to support rather than undermine the creative process is critical for a frogTHINK approach to collaboration. At frog, we typically select a team leader or project manager, whose role is to organize and oversee the collaborative process, to ensure that the atmosphere remains productive and that the team never loses sight of its goals. Timing is critical, too. Ideas don't come in a constant flow, like a stream of water, but arrive in bursts. The leader's responsibility for time management in the collaborative process involves giving the participants time to loosen up and get their minds in the collaborative "groove," and then gauging the quality arc of the ideas that follow.

When a session is managed right, the best ideas start to bubble up after five to ten minutes, and then fade out after twenty to thirty minutes, with participants always being held to the rule that their ideas must have relevance within the "filter" of the objectives set forth for the innovation. When the ideas start to get lame and trivial, the leader stops the session. After a short break, the ideas are presented again, rated, and voted upon. The goal should be for each session to result in three to five interesting ideas. Through the collaborative process, participants' minds grow increasingly freer and more creative, so each new session can address a different and more challenging "problem"—a process of "ideation through irritation."

Although the frogTHINK process isn't set in stone, typically, sessions involve three stages, each of which has a specific time limit and theme. The first stage is about ALTERNATIVES (or free association), which allows participants to start from what they know and then move out in a comfortable exploration of associated ideas. The second stage is RANDOM, and it challenges the participants to push the alternatives further and to consider surprising ideas. The third stage is driven by PROVOCATION or REJECTION, which motivates the innovation team to take its ideas to their extreme—and unexpected—conclusions. In each stage, the team is expected to choose and illustrate at least three good ideas, so that they can be communicated to the other teams. When I conduct these sessions with my design class in Vienna, the minimum time required for each session is one day, and at the end of each session, each ideation team again chooses its three best ideas. All presentations are made to all participants in order to promote mutual inspiration and motivation. One important element of frogTHINK—whether it takes place with my students or in frog's professional collaborations—is unbridled optimism. We avoid using "killer phrases," such as "We've tried this before" or "Management will never go for that," and we instill the belief that change is possible.

It's also critically important to present all of the ideas from these sessions in a professional manner. The more well-developed the presentation, the more qualified the feedback it generates. People who aren't rooted in design can't always make the leap from a pencil sketch to a new kind of piano or a better interaction with a software piece. It's also very important that participants present all ideas and concepts within the brand context, whether that translates to functional principles, the symbolism of the brand, or the national character.

At the end of the ritual phase, the most promising and smartest ideas will continue to thrive in the presence of the "filters" of objectives that surround the innovation process. But you still have more work to do before those ideas are ready for harvesting.

Projection: Envisioning the Innovation's Potential

Although most creative collaborators are eager to share their ideas with as many people as possible—and especially those at the top—this phase of the creative process gives the team an opportunity to first firm up its understanding of the ideas being proposed and how they fit in a larger and more universal context. After the initial ritual phase, participants in the collaborative process must stop to fully explore how the innovation can change the future—for the company, the consumer, and the world.

To understand this phase better, let's revisit the beginning of frog's relationship with KaVo. As I have written before, frog was called in by the dental industry manufacturer to design a new light, but in the end, our company helped KaVo launch a new system of dental equipment that revolutionized the industry, served as the foundation for a new design-based corporate strategy, and reinvigorated the company's brand status.

In 1972 when frog met with the KaVo representatives to discuss new ideas for improving both the visual appeal and ergonomics of the dental environment, German dentists had a high rate of chronic back ailments, which resulted in painkiller and alcohol abuse and ultimately a higher-than-average suicide rate for the profession. In our information-gathering phase (part of the Groundwork I described earlier in the chapter), we spoke with nurses, office workers, and, most importantly, patients, to find out their complaints about and ideas for improving the experience of being in the dentist's office.

We also collaborated with two dental professors, who had precise measurements about stress, muscular wear, and other work-related factors. Everything they said made sense, but their visual examples always showed male dentists and female patients. On a whim, I mentioned that my aunt Wilhelmine Esslinger-Schlachta—a somewhat petite woman—was a dentist, and I asked how many female students they had in their program. They looked perplexed, then smiled somewhat sheepishly as they answered "actually, a lot." In fact, at that time, about 60 percent of the faculty's students were female, and their numbers were growing.

With that revelation, we knew that we needed to leap well beyond the issue of beautification to help KaVo design a plan for real and lasting innovation in their industry. We asked ourselves how our innovation could play out in the future, given the problems we'd learned of and the growing female presence in the profession of dentistry. And then we began collaborating on a new ergonomic framework for KaVo's products.

One of our ideas went to the core of KaVo's business, in an area in which the company held a strategic performance advantage: the design of its air-driven dental instruments. At that time, KaVo produced these tools using computerized machinery, which resulted in very precise, but also very unyielding and "user-unfriendly" metal-cased instruments. Dentists held and manipulated the tools much like they would a pen, and the milled textures on the instruments' surfaces resulted in blistered and callused fingers. We conceptualized a line of instruments with a high-end plastic housing (using the same kind of ABS plastic used in artificial heart valves), which allowed for softer and more ergonomic shapes, while withstanding the high temperatures and aggressive chemicals of sterilization. We also used an elegant array of colors to differentiate the tools and their matching elements by function.

All of these innovations were, in part, designed to appeal to women, which was a strange departure for KaVo's macho culture. But we could show that the dental business would be increasingly driven by female influence, and we could project a future in which our new concept would not only match, but also drive the trend toward more aesthetically *and* ergonomically appealing work environments that would benefit dentists of both sexes. We had imagined how our innovations could change the future—now, we had to gel our ideas and prepare them for presentation to our client.

Management: Getting Everyone Aligned for Action

The final phase of the creative collaboration step involves developing a cohesive picture of the innovative idea and building a plan for supporting and shepherding it toward the third and final step in the process—marketing. I can best illustrate this phase by staying with the example of the new instruments we designed for KaVo.

We prepared all data we could find supporting our case. We also had to overcome some resistance to using plastics in core elements of the instruments (an earlier venture had failed when the plastics used in high-precision valves couldn't stand up to chemicals found in some tap water). We made a solid case for the quality and the long-term sustainability of our concept; the heart valve application and the high cost of ABS convinced even the most critical executive in the meeting. We underscored the fact that women dentists care about aesthetics and wellness, and we collected examples from cosmetics to household products to back up our claim. Finally, we explained that KaVo would be developing a new female-targeted market at a time when that move would put it uniquely in line with the global demographic trend in university dental programs. With that, we had them—and the support we needed.

"Support" at this stage of the innovation chain involves structure, and that includes budget and cash flow—in the right amounts! You can't score big wins when creative strategy and vital innovation needs are treated like commodities. No budget, no results. Although too much money can sometimes muddy the innovative process, all innovators are dependent on money. Not only do they have to have a way to obtain it, but they have to know how to spend it. Most companies have very clearly defined strategies for spending their money, and creative consultants *must* understand the goals and limitations of their client's business plan.

The innovation support structure also involves people—and the right people! Typically, the best person for managing creative projects is a rational, business-minded professional, such as a project manager (or producer, in the case of digital products). In addition to guiding the innovation process, these leaders also are responsible for building and enforcing timelines and performance benchmarks against required specifications. Some of these parameters can be rather complex, especially when you're innovating in medical or other highly technical fields.

Leading the innovation process also requires respect for that process and the creative consultants who contribute to it. In response to the growing body of publications offering case studies and examples of business innovation, many business leaders have turned into semi-experts on approaches to the innovation process. That's not the same thing, however, as having expertise in product development and innovation design (think of it as the difference between having watched a number of heart surgeries and having the hands-on experience necessary to perform the operation yourself). Leaders who fail to make this distinction can waste the time and resources of creative people on their teams and, over time, destroy an organization's innovation culture.

This is the stage during which innovation passes the border between the right and left brain, and it's also where most projects jump the tracks. A simplified "project management," business-as-usual approach alone won't work. Instead, right-brain and left-brain collaborators must engage in a structured cooperative process, guided by strong, rational leadership, but aimed at promoting new ideas and innovative solutions that will build the client's successful future.

○ step 3: marketing (where minds need money)

During this third and final stage of the innovation process, money rules, and that means the collaborative team has to present the answers to some hard financial questions: How does the innovation initiative score in regard to investment and anticipated returns? How does it fare in the market and against its competition? Does its timeline leverage any special opportunities? How is it positioned to overcome barriers of entry and risks? If you think these questions sound difficult to answer, you're right.

Refining and Proving the Innovation's Benefits

Corporate "money people" typically handle more pressure and problems than anybody else in the organization, and many are overwhelmed by the bizarre demands that can come from a business engine beyond their control. Very few financial executives have run a business by themselves, so it's only natural that on occasion they will have trouble accepting the projected returns for a new innovation venture. And, because any investment means "cash out" in addition to deferred tax treatments (translation: taxes go up in the short term), many financial executives are reluctant to buy into any business case built around innovation.

To combat these realities, collaborative teams must have a well-structured plan for proving the innovation's benefits. Creative consultants are likely to lose if they base their arguments on emotion; instead, they must bring hard data to the discussion, analyze similar business cases, and provide some economics-driven options. Begging weakens your position in this situation, and it reflects badly on the strength of the team's leadership. At this point, you need to explore alternatives—find a Plan B—which might mean resigning from the project entirely and taking your ideas with you to form your own company (like Steve Wozniak, who initially offered his design for what would become the Apple computer to his boss at HP). I have on more than one occasion worked for clients with highly cynical CFOs, who asked me what I would do if they rejected the proposal that frog and the client team had worked out. My answer was always something like this: "Just imagine what your competitor would do with this idea—and what that would cost your bottom line within three years." This response has worked on all but a few occasions.

Remember, the CFO doesn't need to be your friend. You're dealing with a strategic thinker and a competent executive, and it is actually healthy if the exchange is as honest and candid as possible. Let your idea be vetted by the toughest standards, and if all parties agree to move forward, the path to success will be easier because of that scrutiny. Many projects die at this stage, but even that end isn't a total loss. If you can't reach an agreement on the proposal, everyone involved will have learned from the process and be better at it next time around.

Collaborative teams need to prepare and argue through this stage as if asking for funding for a start-up. The following list of information points (with compliments to Guy Kawasaki, whom I first met at Apple, and his self-confessed enthusiasm for the top-ten list format) describes the kind of information most venture investors require from a start-up and what you can expect any CFO as an "inside the company investor" to care about when considering whether to fund the marketing of an innovation:

1. The problem and this specific opportunity for addressing it
2. Solution options, based on existing potential or new trends
3. The impact of this innovation on the existing business model (more on this in the next section of this chapter)
4. The organization's underlying talent and technology
5. The marketing and sales plan
6. The competition and risks
7. The launch team's strengths/weaknesses
8. Financial projections and milestones
9. Launch status and timeline
10. The project's summary and call to action

Proving the benefits of your innovation requires a strong focus on Numbers 8 and 9 in this list. Without a detailed understanding of the projected financial costs, milestones, launch status, and timeline, no one can make a sound decision to go forward or kill the project.

Optimizing the Business Model

Most product innovations require changes to the business model as well. Traditional models strive for cheaper products, so any strategy fails when the bottom of that barrel has been reached. You can't starve the cow and still expect it to give milk.

If there is one entrepreneur who truly understands how to integrate the business model and the innovation process, it is Virgin's Richard Branson. The Virgin brand content is a great mix of a superior customer experience with a "New Luxury" focus, combined with an attractive price-to-performance ratio. Virgin's success hinges on tailoring and innovating the business model according to the specific needs and opportunities of each new brand application. Whether it is the upper-class treatment of passengers at Virgin Atlantic or the simplicity of Virgin Mobile's partnership with Target stores, Branson and the Virgin brand managers don't just slap a commodity-like brand on anything that comes along. Instead, they develop an authentic statement for each new venture, which enables them to get a lot of mileage from their brand, while retaining its credibility. To all appearances, the underlying Virgin strategy is to please people and make life fun—profits will follow.

But what about your own innovation challenge? After you have secured a budget and schedule and the innovation team has agreed with the company's high-level executives on the project's overall goals, it's time to discuss with those executives the business model implications of the project. Here, you should proceed in steps. Begin by looking at the company's current strengths and successes and how those can be expanded into new opportunities, with special emphasis on opportunities through your innovation initiative.

To illustrate this process, let's consider the example of Apple and Dell. For many years, Apple was considered the "loser" in the duel between these two rivals. Market share for the Macintosh line—including revenues from the Mac operating system—was minimal for a long time. It took the iPod sensation to propel Apple into a globally dominant position in the field of digital consumer electronics. Even then, Apple still didn't have a dominant online presence—not when compared to Dell, anyway. And it was battling HP, Sony, Panasonic, Samsung, and a host of others for that retail shelf space while simultaneously struggling to succeed in mega-chains, such as Best Buy or Europe's MediaMarkt, that don't have open shelf space. Apple also needed brand control, which most retailers cannot provide.

The solution? Apple adapted its business model to make iTunes the company's online driver. Then, following the examples of Louis Vuitton, Mont Blanc, and Prada, it created the Apple Stores as the keystone of its physical brand experience—one that provides a radically new and extensive customer-service concept. These two steps have helped Apple escape the bare-bones hardware business and enter (even dominate) a different consumer arena—that of high-touch emotions.

How has Dell adapted to these new challenges from Apple? Histori-
cally, Dell has relied on its low-overhead direct mail strategy, which—
with the help of frog—the company converted into a very innovative
eCommerce website, Dell.com. The core of Dell's strategy was providing
built-to-order computers, which allowed the company to deliver just
what the customer really asked for and avoid any waste of systemic over-
featuring. The company coupled this strategy with a huge investment in
supply-chain management systems. Even though much of its hardware
was outsourced, Dell had a very good grip on this model.

Then, systemic innovation struck. As the 1990s progressed, laptops
became more powerful, and desktops and towers fell out of fashion. Laptops involve compressed technology and a frozen set of features—except
for memory and a few minor details, there's nothing "customizable" about
a laptop once it leaves the assembly line in China or Taiwan. The rising
popularity of laptops made Dell's entire business model obsolete.

Without question, Dell still is a great company, and it is making
changes necessary to regain its market share. The company is cutting
costs, it brought Michael Dell back as its CEO in 2007, and it has made
some efforts to upgrade the appearance of its laptops. In addition, the
company is up-marketing new products like digital music players, televisions, and printers. Dell also opened its own stores, but because its
products remain both generic in appearance and nondescript in function,
the stores are really dull. Perhaps Dell could leapfrog the system by connecting its still-superior supply chain with a radical front-end innovation
system where people could design their own products. In any event, Dell
needs to make sure its business model continues to adapt to new marketplace demands.

Given changes in the economy and markets, we finally have a much
more open arena in which to define the best possible business model and
to integrate that model into the overall innovation process. Instead of
asking "Will we be able to sell this?" we can change the question to "How
do we design something that people really want?" And answering that
latter question will involve understanding that people "want" innovative
products, but they also care about the overall ethics and sustainability of
the products' production methods. Increasingly, people want transparency

about any process that involves slave labor, poisonous materials, and excessive carbon emissions, and they also want to know about the end-game of reusability and recycling. Any business model that fails to acknowledge these drivers risks becoming irrelevant in the near future.

In this stage, the innovation initiative or the project finally becomes a "product" or a "solution." The innovation team now must transform into a business unit—or integrate into an existing one. Investments and resources typically begin pouring into the project during this phase, a development that can be simultaneously amazing, scary, and humbling. I always have a lot of butterflies during this stage because it represents a point of no return, with very little opportunity for last-minute refinements. The innovation team must keep things in perspective, stay alert, and make sure that the authentic character of the innovation survives this last stage before market launch. For designers, the ship has left the harbor; they must resist the all-too-frequent temptation to screw up the implementation of the plan by making last-minute requests for changes or rigid demands.

This stage often requires some new collaborative groundwork. In 1997, when frog lead the project to redesign the Lufthansa airline brand experience, our collaboration extended across the organization and beyond. In the years preceding our redesign, I had spent countless hours on Lufthansa's planes, and I always felt that its customer experience was a bit dour. The plane interiors, as well as the check-in areas and lounges, had all the charm of a German Mittelstand office—efficient but boring. When I got a call from Hemjö Klein, who was then a member of Lufthansa's executive board in charge of marketing and brand, with a request to meet and discuss the airline's brand, image, and potential business strategies, I was ready. In our meeting, Hemjö Klein asked me for my ideas—and I had many.

Ultimately, frog's redesign encompassed the entire flight process—making the travel experience with Lufthansa more emotionally engaging and reflective of its rich history and German-Global traditions. We worked especially hard on improving the airport experience. We designed a counter at the check-in area that helps "direct" passengers, while at the same time makes it easier for the agent to maintain good eye contact, manage travel documents, and operate all essential equipment without reaching around awkward barriers. Our design also improved traveler safety by eliminating hidden areas and hollow spaces and by protecting document management and reducing crowds at the desk.

This project also involved infinite details in the plane interiors, from collaborating in the design of more ergonomic and lighter airplane seats (including a comfortable first-class seat that converts to a flat sleeper), to choosing new interior fabrics and leathers, new and lighter tableware, and the wall linings of the airplane interiors. We worked with the potential manufacturers in order to make sure that the price-performance ratio was within the requirements—one of which was to make Lufthansa's renovation of Terminal One at the Frankfurt am Main airport much less expensive than comparable renovation projects at airports such as Charles de Gaulle or Heathrow. And, finally, we redesigned Lufthansa's airport signage.

This project brought us into collaboration with architects, security specialists, contractors, and retailers at the Frankfurt airport. The new airport communication system with digital displays had to be worked out with Philips. The airplane interiors for Airbus and Boeing planes had to be coordinated through Lufthansa's Technik division with a long list of suppliers for the walls, seats, tableware, and more. We had to go back and evangelize the redesign to the flight crews, even though we'd coordinated with their representatives throughout the project. Converting the airport terminal to the new Lufthansa design was relatively easy, but taking older planes out of service for revamping was a costly process that required detailed supervision. At each stage, frog ensured that the implementation of our redesign plan remained firmly in line with our client's central business goals and model. The project was an overwhelming success.

Successful implementation of any design innovation requires that the innovation team fully embrace the goals of its business partner and work to fit these final stages of the process into the company's business model. Mies van der Rohe once said, "God is in the details." But when it comes to making the economics of your innovation work for both the business and its consumers, "God is in the implementation."

Launching the Innovation in the Marketplace

Few tasks demand more resilience and leadership than launching innovative products and ideas to market. Naturally, there are the "usual suspects." Think, for example, of Akio Morita's courageous and competent leadership in launching the Walkman back in 1979, when he personally sold the first 300,000 units to major retailers in the United States and Great Britain. Or consider Steve Jobs' charismatically hip new-product launches. As these global legends have proven, great innovations can't succeed in the marketplace without marketing ingenuity and the support of great leadership.

Success in this stage is defined by totally different and much more traditional parameters than the previous stages. As the innovation enters "public space" and competition, ideas and implementation aren't the only factors that determine its success. Financial backing, competitive strategies (some of them very unfair), conservative markets, and the prevailing economic conditions also play a determining role. As we've seen in other phases of the innovation process, without adequate resources in the launch phase, innovation doesn't have a chance.

But I want to be honest here: Markets aren't always logical places, and not everything works as well as we want it to work. Some brilliant innovations face huge obstacles because consumers still accept dull and utilitarian products, such as ergonomically disastrous laptops or awful user interfaces on mobile devices. For many reasons, bringing a great innovation to market still requires a lot of talent—and a little luck. In this final section of the chapter, I'd like to take a closer look at some market-launch experiences I've had personal involvement in, and the leaders who have excelled at taking bold innovations to market.

o   o   o

Let's begin with Richard Ellenson, a former advertising executive who sold his agency and founded New York-based Blink Twice, Inc. Richard, whose son, Thomas, was born with severe cerebral palsy, founded Blink Twice with the goal of creating a radically improved assisted and augmented communication (AAC) device for children with cerebral palsy. Richard put his money and his life into this new venture, because he understood that speech-generating devices are critical in helping nonverbal individuals reach their potential. Richard wanted to create a device that would help its users build sentences and relationships. He determined that his AAC device should not only help children speak, but it should also motivate others to listen and, in the process, make it easier for teachers, therapists, and parents to support its users. He called his device the Tango.

In 2004, Richard brought his vision to frog and its new parent company, Flextronics. We helped design a perfect vertical integration of specific ergonomics, software, and hardware that improved the ability of children with cerebral palsy to communicate despite their very limited physical abilities. The project involved collaborations with multiple innovative teams. The Tango's groundbreaking Phrase First Language Structure was developed working with Pati King-DeBaun, Dr. Karen Erickson, Caroline Musselwhite, and Patrick Brune. And the Tango's innovative "Two-Hit" spelling keyboard was created in collaboration with Dr. Erickson and Sally Clendon. Linda Burkhart joined Caroline Musselwhite in the creation of Tango Stories, and Linda also developed the device's scanning capabilities. These collaborative ventures have been extremely successful. NIH-funded research has shown that the Tango allows for faster communication and that it boosts the public's perception of its users' abilities—a critical achievement for Richard and his group. (If you'd like a demonstration of these innovations in action, go to www. blink-twice.com. An emulator on that site lets you put the Tango through some of its paces.)

Aside from all of this interrelated collaborative activity, the market launch of the Tango and its promotion as a functional and life-enriching product was a major challenge. Ellenson staged the launch at a conference of the United Cerebral Palsy Association and its adjacent trade show at the LAX Airport Hilton in the spring of 2006. Walking the trade show floor was a depressing experience for all of us. The physical ugliness of products for the disabled is shocking, and most of them are so difficult to use that they challenge the skills of even the most able-bodied humans.

While the people designing and producing these devices may have good intentions, they all seem to ignore the cultural needs of their market—an admittedly narrow market, but one that screams for humanistic designs and solutions. Our admiration for Richard's vision and innovative leadership grew exponentially as we surveyed his competitors' offerings.

Later that evening, we attended a benefit hosted by the United Cerebral Palsy Association, where those of us without a wheelchair were in the minority. Richard delivered an inspiring speech to the Association and the actor William H. Macy delivered a wonderful and very touching keynote address. The true celebrities, however, were the people with cerebral palsy who addressed the gathering using AAC devices—many of them Tangos—giving speeches, performing funny sketches, and even reciting some very romantic poetry.

I'll never forget that evening. These were extremely nice kids—brilliant, highly creative, and passionate people, whose sole means of communicating with other humans and the world was a machine. And the best machine for that job had been envisioned, realized, and brought to market—and to these kids—by Richard Ellenson. When it comes to understanding and equipping the needs of those with cerebral palsy, Ellenson isn't just leading the way of innovation, he and his family are living it.

○ ○ ○

Next, let's consider the launch of enterprise resource planning (ERP) software—the original invention of SAP, one of Germany's few global stars in the digital economy. ERP software is all about mastering the numbers and resources of finance and the supply chain, and its overriding theme is one of logic and rational control. In 1999, when I was asked by co-founder and CEO Hasso Plattner and his product development team (led by Matthias Vering, Leif Jensen-Pistorius, and Peter Hilgers) to help in making the company's software more usable and enjoyable, I saw a wide field of opportunity. The technology of "R/3"—as the software was named back then—was extremely complex, but creativity and design can thrive on adversity. The SAP software developers and designers code-named the project "enjoy," although ultimately the product would be called "mySAP" and "SAPportals."

The project was perfectly managed. Matthias led the inter-corporate collaboration by taking the fear of change away from a group of nearly six hundred developers. Leif and Peter were competent and absolutely ego-free, and Hasso provided the executive inspiration and leadership crucial to any innovation mission. And we were definitely on a mission: The user interface touched about forty thousand different functionalities. The results—as tested by the University of Mannheim, Germany—were impressive. The mySAP applications reduced mistakes by 73 percent and the time-to-learn by 82 percent. Despite the novelty of online applications at that time, SAPportals scored impressively as well, reducing mistakes by 62 percent and time-to-learn by 70 percent. On top of these perfor-mance leaps, the software's user interface looked better than even its strongest competitor's, and it was much more enjoyable to use than the original R/3.

The challenge was to launch it in a way that would appeal to SAP's customers, including the more than one million existing users who might be wary of change and new customers who had to be convinced that mySAP would help to improve their business. At the same time, the product launch had to inspire and convince SAP's global marketing and sales teams. Hasso took on the task himself. As part of the mission, he also asked me to take on a leadership role in SAP's global marketing for one year.

In order to set a global tone and highlight the importance of the U.S. market, we invited members of the global media, along with software gurus, customers, and SAP's leaders to a launch event in Palo Alto, Cali-fornia. Hasso gave a great keynote address and we demonstrated the new software, along with some cool videos we had produced for the occasion. This was a great start for mySAP, but it was just a beginning. We also organized workshops with SAP's local marketing and sales teams around the globe. During these meetings, we improved the relationships between marketing and sales on one side and design and software development on the other. We also met with important customers and took in critical user feedback for on-the-fly improvements of the product.

After a lot of trial and error—and with Hasso's ongoing support—we came up with a series of campaign mottos highlighting some of the "best companies" that use SAP (for example, "Porsche Runs On SAP"), many of which are still in use today. That was in 2000. Nearly a decade later, SAP remains the global leader in ERP software.

o   o   o

Finally, let's look at the launch of Lufthansa's new customer experience— a global initiative that I wrote about earlier in this chapter. This project was as exciting as it was challenging. The project came together and was launched successfully due to good leadership. Hemjö Klein kept Lufthansa's board (led by Chairman and CEO Juergen Weber) up-to-date on the project's plans and progress. We also benefited from ongoing feedback that offered us useful ideas and fantastic support (although some of my non-German colleagues at frog misunderstood these discussions as harsh criticism). To his great credit, Hemjö Klein never made this "his" project. All of the players involved in the project had their say, and all of us shared ownership.

We launched the "New Lufthansa" in one of the major hangars at the Frankfurt am Main airport with a few thousand "Lufthanseates," journalists, and industry personalities from all over the world in attendance. Each team that collaborated on the project showed off and demonstrated its "baby." We updated sections of the cabin with new seats for attendees to test. We also equipped a gate with the new counters and lots of videos to help illustrate and explain the new designs. The ultimate highlight of the launch, however, was the arrival of the first fully configured Boeing 747—named "Victor Alpha"—which had become operational on that very day and was flown in from Lufthansa's Technik Center in Hamburg.

As part of its incredible focus on quality, consistency, and perfection, Lufthansa treated the rollout of the new design like a triple-check of an airplane. New planes went into service with a pristine new look, reconfigured ones were "processed" in accordance with service cycles, as was the remodeling of airport areas under Lufthansa's control. Lufthansa's innovative design has established the airline as a global leader, and has helped expand the boundaries of airline design. But it took a carefully orchestrated and managed rollout of these innovations to make them succeed with Lufthansa's board, employees, and customers.

o o o

As these examples have shown, innovation paired with culture and a love for usability is a timeless formula for success. These companies and their leaders have succeeded in bringing innovative convergent products and customer experiences to market with very tight funding and the smart use of resources. If you need proof of the critical importance of good leadership and a well-tuned innovation process, just compare the results-to-investment ratio of these game-changing innovation launches to the millions of dollars spent by some companies to introduce mere incremental product changes to the market.

The examples and stories offered here also underscore an important point contained in the title of this chapter: When it comes to successfully designing and marketing innovation, minds beat money every time. The innovative process can't succeed without creative, collaborative participants and strong, visionary leadership. From the important groundwork at the onset of the innovation process to managing the creative collaboration and providing the guidance necessary to launch the innovation in a competitive, global arena, the "human factor" plays a deciding role in the project's eventual success. Yes, innovation requires money, but without the participation of brilliant minds, few innovations can succeed—no matter how much money is behind them.

5

a business design revolution
the greening of planet, inc.

*"Even if I knew that tomorrow the world would go to pieces,
I would still plant my apple tree."*
—Martin Luther

Let's be honest. Design, like marketing, is about driving mass consumption, and anything produced on a mass scale contributes to pollution and global warming. That makes designers and their business clients systemic players in an economic model that has a profound effect on the environment. According to traditional business reasoning, the more items we send flying off the production line, the better our chances for economic success. But now we've realized that the traditional indicators of economic success might not have been giving us the whole story. We've seen the powerful influence of design on the business model and how strong leadership shapes and implements creative, innovation-driven strategies to achieve more sustainable profitability. But we also have to understand that design's role in building sustainability extends well beyond the profits of individual enterprises.

All of those "cheap" goods that we've churned out have proven themselves to be much too expensive culturally, socially, and environmentally—in fact, they're killing us—and "green thinking" finally has become a mainstream political and economic issue. Today, governments around the world have joined forces, admitting that our thoughtless destruction of the earth's environment has created an immense—and manmade—problem. Now, we can only hope that our human intellect and ingenuity will be up to the task of solving that problem and saving the planet. The growing movement toward eco-capitalism isn't an exercise in "do-goodism." It's driven by self-preservation, and it demands a rapid change of course in our approach to production and consumption.

One of our most powerful methods for achieving that shift is to reshape the industrial process. Designers and their collaborative business partners have a great opportunity to affect the strategic early stage of the product lifecycle management (PLM) system. In fact, we *must* define an economic strategy in that early stage if we want the strategy to be effective. This kind of up-front process change is good business. By changing the industrial process model from one designed to support mass efficiency to one designed to promote socially and environmentally responsive innovation—say, for example, by incorporating environmentally sound methods and materials right into our process model—we can increase the value of a company and improve its sales.

This important shift requires a change in the way companies work and in the way they interact and collaborate with their customers. We have to innovate business models so that customers join executives, employees, and owners/shareholders on equal footing as "caretakers" of businesses and the world they serve.

Designers, whose work forms the interface between humans and science, technology, and business, have the obligation and opportunity to shape the drivers of the new "green" economy, and we at frog have been on the front lines of that effort. Knowing that we are all part of a very complex system, frog has pursued multiple tactical approaches to achieving its strategic goal of greening the global consumer-tech industry. Our approach involves analyzing and adapting processes in product strategy, planning, design, engineering, and production, as well as the corresponding operative support, consumption/use, and recycling stages of the product life cycle.

In this chapter, I'll offer ideas for implementing environmentally sound solutions at every stage of product life cycle, but with special emphasis on the early stages of the industrial design and manufacturing processes. Along the way, I'll share with you the options we've developed for changing the current industrial paradigm of "cheap, cheaper, poisonous" to one of better business, stronger profits, and better value for all of us.

○ designing early-stage solutions

We humans have been polluting and poisoning the earth for many years, but our search for a better way of using our resources is still in its infancy. Most current green efforts, such as recycling, still address only the *effects* of reckless production and consumption, rather than the causes.

Europe has a long and healthy green tradition, and designers and industrialists from other parts of the world might be able to model some of their own solutions on its initiatives. European legislation, for example, sets better standards for recycling in industrial products by creating rules that make recycling easier—rules such as those that prohibit manufacturers from gluing two different materials together or from painting plastics, for example. But even in Europe, there is still an overwhelming focus on the very last stage of the product lifecycle, leaving a clear need to manage environmental impact at the top of the PLM chain. The environmental sustainability of our products and processes can best be addressed through better strategic choices and early stage design.

The American automobile industry is a prime example of what happens when business strategists fail to consider the early stages of the lifecycle management of their products. It's also one of the largest contributors to greenhouse gasses in the world, making it the focus of government regulation and technological innovation. Traditionally, American automobile manufacturers have conceptualized, designed, and produced cars with the main objectives of having the best sales performance at the lowest manufacturing cost. In spite of environmentalists' warnings and political and legislative pressure from California and other states, it took the near meltdown of the economy to force America's "Big Three" automakers to seriously pursue the development of environmentally responsible automobiles. The industry's reluctance to become good environmental citizens sooner—rather than later—was bad business for them, for the American economy, and for the American people. And that bad business was rooted in bad design.

Consumers, of course, can't be expected to detect the seeds of environmental danger present in the early stages of a product's development. The physical effects of pollution and waste that come about later in a product's lifecycle—in its usage phase—are more visible, and therefore the perceived impact of late-stage problems is greater. That's why the grass roots environmental movement began as an effort to reduce and regulate pollution, as well it should have. The effects of dangerous pesticides or smoke stack emissions are much easier to grasp than are the design flaws that created those problems in the first place. Incorporating environmental protections into the front end of the industrial process—while designs and strategic goals are still in development—is not only more complex, but it requires methods that are less generally understood. And it requires a focus on *future* growth and sustainability, rather than on short-term profits.

Today, with the United States joining other nations in accepting the challenge of transforming into a green economy, designers and innovative business leaders have to focus on changes that lie within their power. To realize those changes, we'll have to prove that green industrial strategies result in better business—and more of that other kind of "green" that businesses so avidly seek.

To understand the strategic opportunities for ecologizing industrial production in today's globally networked environment, let's look at all four stages of the industrial product lifecycle and how they apply to consumer technology products. In essence, here is what each of those stages involves:

Stage 1—product genesis: strategy and design

Stage 2—production: applying materials, consuming energy, emitting pollutants

Stage 3—usage: consuming materials, consuming energy, emitting
 pollutants

Stage 4—recycling: reuse of materials, management of disposed
 waste

Our most effective opportunity for ecological intervention occurs in
Stage 1, where we can devise strategies that eliminate pollution and waste
before a penny has been invested in materials or physical resources.
Taking advantage of that opportunity, however, requires farsighted and
innovative business models. That means we have to push for a more
proactive, less wasteful, and more socially ethical approach to industrial
planning, production, usage, and recycling. We have to be smarter and
do more with less. We at frog, along with designers and business leaders
around the world, have developed some ideas for accomplishing those
goals. Let's look at some of those ideas.

○ developing green business strategies

Of course, no business executive will switch strategies without sound
economic reasons for doing so. The good news—if there is any to be
found—in the worldwide economic upheaval has been that it has has-
tened the collapse of most "low-cost" strategies and their poisonous,
boring output of useless stuff that nobody needs or wants. The growing
concern for worker safety and rights in areas such as China, India, South-
east Asia, and Eastern Europe also has dimmed the financial outlook for
strategies relying solely on cheap labor. The recall of millions of toxic
children's toys that were made in China and revelations about melamine
used as filler in pet foods and infant formula has caused a further backlash against "cheap" goods that, in these cases, cost lives.

Wal-Mart, Fisher-Price, and other major retailers are revising their
business strategies and reversing the momentum toward shelves stuffed
with cheap, toxic imports. In several interviews, the chairman and CEO
of Toys-R-Us, Gerald Storch, who was also one of the successful builders of
Target stores, explained in detail what retailers and the industry are doing
to make toys safer. He also made a point of saying that green products

sold well in 2007, "though there weren't a lot in the marketplace." He expects to see a dramatic expansion in green-based products in the years to come.

We need a paradigm shift for all global consumer businesses—and especially for American industry. For this kind of paradigm shift to occur, we have to accept the new challenges facing us and use them as an opportunity to accomplish positive change. That will mean advancing our professional goals in the strategic early stage of the industrial process, but we also have to improve our ethics. As designers *and* consumers, we have to stop supporting environmentally harmful industries and businesses and become active partners in forging our own environmental destiny.

As creative strategists and designers, our objectives should be to foster green thinking in the companies we deal with while also creating concepts that can help our clients achieve long-term, sustainable success with green initiatives. This kind of design-driven green revolution may sound like wishful thinking, but it can and does work—and there are several successful models to prove it.

In the 1990s, Germany began building an effective recycling program to preserve valuable natural resources, and it has gone on to become a very positive and profitable business, as was proven when Kohlberg Kravis Roberts & Co. (KKR)—a private equity leader and majority shareholder in frog's current parent company, Aricent—acquired Germany's largest recycling company, Der Gruene Punkt (The Green Point). At the same time, Germany launched a major drive to promote sustainable technologies by encouraging government-subsidized investments in clean tech companies. Many of these companies are in the former East Germany, so the nation's investment in those industries also helped with its reunification.

Germany's Chancellor Angela Merkel sees conservation as an ecological principle as well as an ideological one. As a result, the German economy advances and promotes green technologies and behaviors, which in return results in new green industries and new business opportunities. The country has achieved a global leadership position in photovoltaic (PV) solar cell production, distribution, installation, and use. The government is also tackling the hidebound practices of the country's very powerful automobile industry, forcing its members to go "green" or go out of business (the pressure from prime export markets like California helps make the case). As a first step, the government has empowered cities to ban polluting cars, especially those with old and unfiltered diesel engines. As a result, German automakers are forging ahead in the development (and subsequent success) of developing green automotive technology.

Now let's compare this success with the United States' experiment with such environmental legislation and the economic opportunities it offers. And for that, we'll return to the story of the American automotive industry and its response to California's quest for zero emission vehicles (ZEVs). In 1990, the California Air Resources Board adopted regulations requiring that each year, from 1998 and through 2003, increasing percentages of cars sold within the state of California were to be ZEVs. Instead of recognizing this as a major opportunity to create a new market for ground-breaking innovation, General Motors, Ford, and Chrysler (the Big Three) vehemently protested and lobbied against the measure and eventually were joined in their cause by the federal government (under the Bush Administration). Ultimately, after a massive drain of legislative time and lobbying dollars, the legislation was diluted to the point that it became irrelevant. As a result, technological innovation in the area of ZEVs came to a standstill, and American automakers simply continued to produce the same gas-guzzling designs that choke the air, contribute to global warming, and cause conflicts with oil-rich nations overseas.

So how did things work out for the automotive manufacturers who made the strategic decision to let the green train pass them by? Bill Ford certainly made some efforts toward environmentally responsible change, including his green initiatives in rebuilding the Rouge industrial complex in Dearborn, Michigan, with environmental architect William McDonough. And he brought frog in to design the electric city car and its digital navigation components. He intended to pioneer the car through his Ford TH!NK project but, unfortunately, the company wasn't able to make the cultural shift necessary to design and launch such a revolutionary product. The TH!NK project deteriorated into a dismal failure. In the end, it produced little more than a better golf cart. Ford sold the TH!NK project and IP to the Norwegian firm, Kamcorp, and that company is making nice progress on the project. Hopes are high for the results, especially given the new imperative for fuel efficiency and reduced emissions.

Ultimately, however, Bill Ford had to step aside, and in 2006, the former CEO at Boeing, Alan Mulally, came on to launch another "turnaround." He inherited some problems, however. Ford continued to produce the Explorer SUV, an automobile that has been subject to several claims of flawed safety. And the company Mulally inherited also owned a collection of European luxury brands, all but one of which (Volvo) were considered by many to be on the decline. Mulally soldiered on by attempting to integrate these brands into the Ford system, rather than using some of their European manufacturing groups as innovation pods for developing and testing new technologies. The Volvo brand—known for its quality and safety—would have been a credible trailblazer for environmentally sound mobility. Aston Martin could have developed a model powered by a fuel cell engine—a move that would have offered a bold statement. Instead, these European acquisitions were just another money drain, and Mulally offered them up to the chopping block during the Congressional automotive bailout hearings of November 2008.

Finally, Chrysler went through the DaimlerChrysler corporate rollercoaster. This merger went wrong from the start—in other words, in its early stages of strategy and planning. German and American engineering methods and business processes are relatively incompatible, and no one involved in the merger created a strategy for bridging that cultural and operational gulf. Daimler-Benz and its board were naïve about the follow-up risks and cost of the Chrysler merger. And Chrysler's Robert Eaton was looking for a safe haven for a company that had succeeded at maintaining profitability, but had no future strategy or goals. You wouldn't have known that, of course, listening to Juergen Schrempp of Daimler-Benz speak glowingly about the merger to CNN: *"Today we are creating the world's leading automotive company for the 21st century. We are combining the two most innovative car companies in the world."* Lack of strategy, poorly thoughtout process issues, and a total absence of creativity or innovation doomed this merger and cast a bleak shadow over the future of the company.

The merger didn't fix Chrysler's problems. Its vehicles continued to be too large, too fuel-hungry, and too out-of-step with today's buyers. Again, the company had opportunities to step up into the 21st century. In 2003, frog was brought in to design an experimental interior for a light truck under the Dodge brand. We created some really meaningful features, which would have made driving both safer and more fun, including a truck bed that owners could easily reconfigure to accommodate tailgating parties, and a digital media system that would have enabled drivers and passengers to take full advantage of new media technologies. Even though our concept was absolutely in line with the company's own user research, which showed that people weren't happy with the Dodge truck's interior and dour functionality (some called it a "utilitarian turn-off"), it didn't make the cut. And Dodge sales continued to plummet.

When Juergen Schrempp finally stepped down in 2005, he left behind a company with shares worth 50 percent of their pre-merger value and an additional eighty thousand people out of work as a direct or indirect result of this incredible mismanagement. In 2007, Daimler-Benz, which originally acquired Chrysler for $36 billion, sold 80 percent of the company for $7.4 billion to private equity firm Cerberus Capital Management. To make the deal happen, Daimler also paid Cerberus about $650 million in cash for "associated liabilities." All told, the merger, mismanagement, and "un-merger" cost Daimler shareholders nearly $30 billion. Just imagine what kind of green technology advancements Mercedes Benz—Daimler's star brand—could have made with just a fraction of that $30 billion in evaporated assets.

But from all of this disaster came some good news. Ecology-driven innovation—such as energy-saving or zero-emission vehicles—now makes economic sense. GM Europe accelerated its efforts to launch a line of cars powered by fuel cells and began publicly testing its fourth pre-series generation. GM also revived its concept of an all-electric vehicle, a project the company had killed early in its development. If all goes as scheduled, the Volt will be available for drivers in 2010 or 2011, as long as enough safe lithium-ion batteries are available—a condition that offers its own challenges.

No matter how you slice it, all three American automakers failed as businesses because they failed to devise a more innovative and creative strategic approach to their businesses and products. Instead of providing their customers with products offering higher quality, better environmental sustainability, and improved safety—three proven elements to long-term financial success—the Big Three succumbed to cynical compromises, outdated technology, and obsolete concepts. They failed as businesses because their leaders failed as strategists to respond to the growing and quite evident global demand for more environmentally responsible and sustainable products.

○ monitoring the ecological load factor of new products and technologies

In every industry, crafting a sound ecological strategy and design requires the critical leadership skill of foresight. Not only do we need to envision what people will do and experience with a new product, but we have to show what the eventual mass production, use, and recycling of that product will mean to the environment. On top of that, we have to understand and communicate what the implementation of systemic technology innovations will mean for society and humankind. As an example, consider the implications of the proliferation of nuclear power plants. What are the potential dangers of their operation? Can we monitor how those plants, with their potential for plutonium enrichment, are being used by fascist states? These are questions that must be answered if we want to safely pursue this technology as an alternative energy source. And these are the types of questions we must ask ourselves about any technology, manufactured product, or manufacturing process.

In our lifetime, the Internet may rank as the technology that has most influenced society, and it offers a prime example of the complexities involved in determining the environmental impact of new products or technologies. Because of its ability to break down communication barriers, the Internet has influenced global trade, with both good and bad outcomes. By facilitating global trade, the Internet has made outsourcing easier, which has brought devastating competition for small retail business and has turned many small-city downtowns into ghost towns (not to mention the fact that increased global manufacturing has dramatically increased levels of resource use, industrial waste, and post-consumer trash). On the other hand, the Internet also has facilitated long-distance communication and improved knowledge-gathering and global collaboration, and these very advancements may carry the key to finding answers to individual and industrial resource use and waste reduction. This capability has forever changed the scientific assessment and monitoring of industrial production.

The scientific watch-dogging of products and technologies started in the United States. From 1972 to 1995 the Congressional Office of Technology Assessment (OTA) was the nonpartisan analytical agency that assisted Congress with increasingly complex and highly technical issues that might have had an effect on American society. OTA's first assignment, for example, was to research the effects of the pesticide DDT. The U.S. Congress created the entity because it wanted more qualified information and a holistic projections for future technologies before making any decision for the greater good of the country. The OTA no longer exists (after it closed, its research was acquired by Princeton University), but its original goals offer a good platform for us to explore how we, as designers and executive strategists, can implement ecological values in our work and thereby help reduce the environmental impact of new technologies and their development. Today, Germany leads the world in studying the effects of technology on nature and society. The German Parliament has set up a bipartisan office for *Technikfolgen-Abschaetzung* or "Research About the Effects of Technology" (called TA) in its lower house, with this stated mission: *"By analyzing and anticipating opportunities and risks—including eventual, non-intended side-effects—which a new technology will bring to society and environment, TA contributes to the design, guidance, and control of technological developments."*

Technology monitoring takes into account a number of social and environmental issues. TA researchers look at how new technologies are created, and they consider the scientific and social elements driving these creations. For example, increased airline security and bionic supervision of large crowds is clearly driven by the threat of terrorism. The current race for greener energy sources also is being driven by security concerns—we buy most of our oil from nations hostile to us—as much as it is by social and environmental ones. By monitoring the social and environmental impact of technologies involved in the products and processes we design, we can offer businesses, their shareholders, and their customers better products, higher profits, and increased value.

Implementing an ELF Rating System

As designers, creative consultants, and business strategists, it is part of our job to help companies recognize where green opportunities lie. And, by building green strategies into the early phases of the product and process lifecycle, we can better manage all four phases of that cycle. We also can create a strategic environment that enables near total freedom of thinking in the earliest planning phase. We can begin this process by carefully assessing the materials involved in creating common technology products to determine what I call their "ecological load factor," or ELF. In addition to measuring a product's environmental impact, ELF ratings would also measure the emotional impact that product has on consumers, with the assumption that consumers feel good about owning and using products that don't pollute or that benefit the environment in other ways.

By adding an "industrial ecology" element to the product life cycle—one that underscores the truth that waste is always a drag on profits—a solid ELF process will change the way we design and manufacture products, as well as the way we market, purchase, use, and dispose of them. Internal marketing efforts will have to adapt to this new paradigm, beginning with a move from passive mass marketing and "one-shot" sales to more personal customer relationships in which services supersede physical sales, both in importance and revenue. ELF ratings also will motivate, reward, or fine consumers for their product purchase and use decisions. A product that might be considered cool or "a good buy" in today's marketplace may have a different value rating once consumers recognize (and have to pay for) its not-so-good ELF performance. And that outcome will affect business revenues, as well as the environment.

The idea of measuring ELF is similar to the concept of life cycle assessment (LCA). In that process, companies try to pinpoint the source of a material, how it gets to the manufacturing plant, how it's used in the manufacturing process, and what happens to it at the end of its life (recycle, reuse, or waste). Based on the cost of each of those stages, the product receives an LCA score between 1 and 100, with lower scores equaling lower costs. Like LCA ratings, ELF ratings can range from 1 to 100, but that score also would reflect an assessment of the product's emotional value for consumers. The lower the ELF score, the more ecologically friendly and emotionally fulfilling a product would be rated.

Of course, this rating system is still just a proposal. The task for strategic-creative consultants and their business collaborators is to provide the tools that can make the ELF scoring system effective and impartial. It's also vital to integrate some form of environmental-load factoring scores into databases, so that corporate strategists, designers, engineers, manufacturers, buyers, and consumers can have universal access to relevant information about given products and processes, at any time and place.

Another challenge for any effort such as ELF is to find a way to define, publish, and manage rating guidelines so that they reflect a standardized metric and can, therefore, have a relevant financial impact. In my opinion there are many good systems in place that grade a variety of elements in the industrial process: ISO 9000, for example, defines standards for the quality and consistency of products, services, and processes; DIN (German industry norm) does the same for functional and qualitative compliance; TUV (German Technology Supervision Association) does it for recycling compliance. In the United States, the Energy Star program rates appliance efficiency, and the American UL standards warrant the safety and robustness of electrical products. And organizations such as Skryve (www.scryve.com) and Vanno (www.vanno.com) have begun early efforts to provide a ratings system for gauging a company's environmental responsibility and the sustainability of their product models.

In other words, while establishing global ELF rating standards, reporting, and monitoring practices would be a major undertaking, it can be done. And the results could be enormous for manufacturers, consumers, and the environment. We talk more about this and other challenges later in the chapter. For now, let's look more closely at how ELF standards could impact the product life cycle and explore some strategies for putting those standards to work—right away.

Why Wait? Pursuing ELF Strategies

We don't have to wait for an official rating system to begin improving the environmental load factor of our products and processes. And one way that strategic-creative consultants could help their clients leapfrog competitors in this process is to incorporate convergent technologies in their designs. The marketplace has already shown that consumers are interested in products that offer combined uses, brands, and strategies—consider, for example, the mobile phone, which is, in fact, a computer with a minimized display and interface. With different modular sensors, this kind of multi-functional device can be extended to offer personal safety features, medical monitoring, or any number of customizations. In addition to saving resources, cost, and materials, the advantage to a strategic approach based on convergent technology will lead to a better usage ratio of technology, better functionality, and a more universal connectivity in the virtual back-end.

Making high-tech products more modular is another way to build a strategic-ecological approach to design and manufacturing. Instead of discarding an entire product because of a malfunction in one of its minor components, our products should have functional parts that can be updated or replaced individually. This isn't a radical idea, of course. Even a few decades ago, electronic and appliance repair shops could be found in almost any town or city in the United States, before the common wisdom dictated that it was "cheaper" to toss anything broken or slightly out-of-date into the landfill.

Modularity also makes good environmental (and economic) sense because many components—especially those of digital-analog convergent products—have different lifecycle and innovation potential. Let's take medical products as an example: The physical elements—the casing, wires, and so on—may "live" for five to ten years, but the digital elements may need to be updated every eighteen months, to avoid becoming obsolete. Further, until recently, nearly all medical products were designed as integral digital concepts. But newer product designs, especially in diagnostic equipment, separate the components responsible for the sensing and the processing of data so that individual elements can be updated as necessary. There is no real reason why consumer products like music players or mobile phones shouldn't offer the same upgradable design.

We could gain enormous environmental benefits from upgradable designs. For example, as much as my iPhone or my BlackBerry are convergent and useful devices, they aren't yet recyclable by state-of-the-art standards for complete disassembly. Nor are any of the cheaper mobile phones out there. Every year, there are almost one billion of these devices produced, and every year, almost six hundred million phones are thrown away—most in the United States alone. That means telecommunication companies together with the phone manufacturers—and users—are responsible for quite a stash of environmentally damaging trash. This mountain range of toxic detritus is starting to become a money issue for some businesses. In Europe, for example, the European Union requires manufacturers and sellers to take back any product that doesn't comply with new and stringent disassembly standards. Other nations could use this kind of legislation as well. But in the meantime, every business can begin to take its own steps toward increasing technical modularity and thereby decreasing the ELF rating of new products.

Another way to jump-start the move toward designing products with lower ELF ratings is to reduce the use of resources across the board—in factories, transport, logistics, sales, usage, repair, and recycling. This is an ecological approach to strategy and design that makes economic sense, both for producers and for users. Consumers are more aware than ever before of the importance of environmentally responsible products and production methods. Enabling them to choose products that have a low ELF rating makes consumers part of the solution to global warming and pollution reduction, and it provides them with a more rewarding and emotionally rich consumer experience.

All of these methods are achievable, but as I've stated before, the only way to adopt an ecological strategy is with an open mind and a commitment to building environmental concerns into the early design phase of product development. By doing that, you can drive change and profitability throughout the cycle, to include the product's sales, use, and reuse or recycling. These changes provide powerful marketing and sales tools that go well beyond the sometimes wasteful and unproductive "brute force" approach of clogging the marketplace with multiple versions of the same old thing.

○ overcoming the challenges of going green

Building a new business paradigm is a huge goal, but happily, it's just the kind of challenge that speaks to the human spirit. In spite of our undeniable drive toward self-preservation—and self promotion—we love to band together to build new things.

Designing and implementing new strategic approaches to business and industrial production isn't a simple task, but the drive to find shared solutions for achieving shared goals has held true for every society throughout time. But understanding and mitigating all of the potential environmental fallout from any product's manufacture and use is a complex undertaking. As a result, manufacturers face particularly big challenges in implementing environmental considerations in their business model—challenges that require innovative solutions.

Leveraging the Money Motive

We humans are very fond of money, and overcoming our desire for "cheap" solutions represents a critical challenge for businesses attempting to implement green strategies. In seeking to answer this challenge, businesses first must weigh the potential costs and benefits of any "green" initiative. To understand the complexity of that process, let's consider the example of the hybrid and electric car industry.

When we look at all the process elements of the Toyota Prius or the Tesla Roadster, we soon discover that these cars aren't quite as "green" as one might think. The batteries that help power both the Prius and the Roadster come from a very "dirty" technology, with complex chemical hazards involved in their creation and subsequent recycling. True, because of their reduced greenhouse gas emissions, the ELF of these cars is still much better than that of conventional automobiles. But the Toyota

Prius still has a gasoline engine, and the all-electric Tesla still requires a plug to recharge. Let's also remember that electricity isn't as clean as some people think, either. Many electrical power plants are fueled with coal—and you can forget anything anyone ever said to you about "clean coal." With whole ranges of the Appalachian mountains being blown up to get at this energy source, and the water, air, and soil pollution that results (not to mention the loss of homeland and habitat), there's nothing clean about coal—or the electricity it generates. And the ELF of nuclear power plants isn't great, either, given the potential for nuclear disasters and the unavoidable issue of nuclear waste.

So what about fuel cells? Fuel cells are three times as efficient as internal combustion engines, and with zero carbon emissions, the technology is too good to pass up. Every major car manufacturer in the world is in the advanced testing stages of zero-emission fuel cell automobiles, but that doesn't mean this technology will save the auto industry. Although the technology behind fuel cells has been known and used for decades, there are still quite a few technological hurdles to overcome before they hit the auto market. Most current automotive designs require several cells in order to provide enough electricity to power the car. But a standard-sized tank filled with 4.5 kilograms of pressurized hydrogen is only good for a range of about 350 km or 220 miles (which is why most concepts combine fuel cells with an electric buffer battery). Also, the water inside the fuel cells boils at 100 degrees C. On a hot and sunny day, the water can boil away completely, causing the cell to lose conductivity. Fuel cells require a constant flow of liquids going into and out of the cell, and those liquids remain difficult to control.

I don't go through this litany of environmental considerations to convince you that it's simply impossible to produce an environmentally sustainable means of transportation. On the contrary, even with the environmental issues that remain for fuel cell technology, its absolute zero emission of greenhouse gasses and its reduced dependence on fossil fuels makes fuel-cell technology a solid candidate for new engines. But it's important to remember that, like all necessary undertakings, implementing green goals in our creative strategies requires concentrated effort and

the combined talents and attention of business leaders, creative consultants, consumers, and—not least of all—our governments. The complexity of this task makes it expensive, and it requires an up-front investment
for long-term profitability. And it's an investment that *all* of us will have
to make.

Money rules the world, and in this case, money will have to save the
world. When Congress asked the Big Three automakers why they had
continued to crank out fuel-wasting SUVs instead of investing in new
fuel-efficient and alternative technologies, the automakers responded by
saying that they only gave the American public what it wanted. To some
extent, that might be true, and that's why we have to offer consumers real
incentives for "wanting" products that won't destroy the planet. In other
words, products with a bad ELF rating will have to cost lots of money,
and products with a good EFL rating will need to be more profitable for
manufacturers and a better value for consumers.

2008 gave us a marvelous example of the power of the money motive
in curbing dangerous personal choices. In July of that year, oil was selling
for just shy of $150 a barrel and consumers around the United States were
reeling under gas prices approaching $5 a gallon. People parked their
SUVs in the front yard with "For Sale" signs in the windows. Drive-
through lanes were suddenly clear, as people walked inside to do business. Public transportation use went up, as did car pooling and other
rational (but previously unpopular) forms of fuel economy. Demand for
better public transportation rose along with air quality, and the wealthy
Texas oil and gas man, T. Boone Pickens, made the rounds of talk shows
to explain his plans to build wind farms across the United States to end
the nation's dependence on foreign oil. And, as demand for oil weakened,
its price edged downward.

By October, the world economy was in full meltdown, and oil prices
plummeted. People in the United States—at least those who hadn't had
their automobiles repossessed—developed oil price amnesia and hopped
back behind the wheel. Driving distances went up again, as did America's
tolerance for its dependence on foreign oil. And what about those wind
farms? Pickens announced that his plans would be delayed, due to

reduced interest in finding alternative energy solutions. So, in fewer than six months, we were able to see just how quickly Americans could adjust to using less fuel, how reduction in use was directly linked with a reduction in cost (and a reduction in pollution), and how immediately the promise of investment could promote quite aggressive plans for producing alternative energy. Unfortunately, we also saw how quickly we can forget the goals of efficiency, environmental protection, and national security when we don't have a money motive prompting us to remember them. In America, at least, money remains the most effective catalyst for change, and innovators will need to find ways to leverage the "money motive" in any green business strategy.

Joining Forces

Enacting change through well-researched innovations and strategically applied economic pressure takes a concerted effort. Happily, we designers and business leaders won't be alone in our commitment to pursuing environmentally sustainable business strategies. There are plenty of organizations, such as Greenpeace and the Sierra Club, that have long histories of developing such strategies and pursuing the goal of protecting our natural environment.

But, while such organizations come quite close to the political and social core issues that would be addressed by enacting an ELF rating system, even they haven't proposed grading industrial products in the same way some organizations grade, certify, and rate other commodities, such as organic foods. What kind of progress toward environmentally sustainable industrial models might we make, if we could combine the power of existing environmental programs with operational programs governing global industrial quality, standards, and compliance? With that kind of cooperative effort, we could create and/or aggregate relevant industrial ELF information, based on full-cycle process information that currently is unavailable or poorly tracked and managed.

Without question, any large-scale industrial/ecological effort would spawn "political" lobbying and bickering, and many industries and companies would try to pay their way out of compliance. In the end, however, businesses that fail to incorporate environmental concerns into their strategic plans are destined to become the pariahs of the world—and to fail. The urgent need and the growing demand for environmentally responsible industrial, business, and consumer practices is never going to disappear, because the world has forever lost its environmental innocence. We know what we have to do; we just have to figure out the best way to do it. And those businesses that invest in green strategies now will be better positioned for success today, tomorrow, and into the future. Those that fail to change will be kicked to the environmental curb.

The same goes for countries that don't change or commit to environmental treaties—as has happened in the United States. To return to a position of world leadership, America is finally recognizing that it has to live up to the humanistic ideals penned by its founding fathers. The United States needs to become a good and shining example again. Becoming more responsible world citizens will be good for American businesses, too. The green economy is on its way, and the businesses that are ready to participate in it will be global winners.

We only have one last chance left to stop the earth's ecological meltdown, and it requires that we change the behavioral patterns and principles that dominate our current economic and industrial systems. Instead of a cold and egotistical capitalism that almost always includes excessive and quite often ruthless individualism, we need to implement a warmer, more collective, and socially responsible model of economic behavior. That means we have to change our attitudes about industry and demand that it serve and preserve humanity, not the other way around. We—you and I and everyone who shares our world—are responsible for realizing that change. As Mahatma Gandhi said, "*You must be the change you wish to see in the world.*"

Overcoming Industrial-Cultural Colonialism

In 1959, when I was a fifteen-year-old exchange student at the Lycee de Garcons in Montlucon, France, I had my eyes opened to the problems of colonialism—the problems that result when one country or culture attempts to impose its ideas, values, and beliefs on another, and exploits

its resources along the way. In the late 1950s, France was struggling to appease its immigrant population while trying to calm explosive upheavals in its colonies in Algeria and Indo-China (the situation in Laos and Cambodia was especially dire at that time and eventually led to the Vietnam War). It was during this time that, while traveling on the night train from Strasbourg to Lyon, I shared my space with a group of young French soldiers on their way to join the fighting in Algeria. Their fear and anger were palpable, and they all got very drunk with French wine—as did I.

As I listened to these young soldiers describe what to them seemed a bitter but quite necessary effort to bring France's colonies "into line," I couldn't help but recall the other voices I'd heard speaking of this struggle in my adopted hometown. Montlucon was home to a number of Algerian and Indo-Chinese refugees, and I often had heard their first-hand accounts of shocking acts on the part of the French "occupiers" as well as the revenge by resistance guerillas—stories of brutal repression and fear. Our French teachers told us that France's colonies were a curse both for the French and for the people of the distant lands it sought to control. The people in the colonies wanted independence and peace, but they could not have it unless France could achieve some kind of an economic and strategic advantage from "its" colonies. Sadly, not much has changed in that part of the world, except that now, such exploitation takes place at the hands of bankers and industrialists, rather than military commanders and government officials.

Today, "industrial-cultural colonialism" represents one of the biggest obstacles designers and business leaders must overcome in creating environmentally responsible product strategies. For years, Americans, Western Europeans, and the Japanese have moved their factories to third-world countries where labor is cheap and regulations governing industrial production are few—and often toothless. And, of course, when Western countries move industrial production into the third world, they also expect to open up new markets in those areas for the low-cost products they're churning out. As we know, this industrial paradigm has been dismal and destructive for everyone involved. And it has forced some particularly difficult and disheartening realities upon designers.

When I worked with Sony thirty years ago, we were very aware of the wide variety of cultural and fashionable "tastes" around the world. We also knew that, to successfully reach international markets, Sony's product concepts had to respect the aesthetics and traditions of other local cultures. We called our product design "international style," and we meant it to be adaptive. The underlying product architecture of our designs may have been based on a common system, but a television designed for Brazil looked quite different from one designed for Great Britain, Saudi Arabia, Nigeria, or Malaysia. We rejected the "wood grain and brass" style that dominated American consumer electronics back then, because we felt that a people capable of sending men to the moon would be open to more progressive aesthetics. We were right. We also were fortunate enough to have the backing of strong, visionary leadership.

Today's mass culture is no longer defined by leaders like the ones we worked with at Sony or Apple. Global mass culture is formed by international supply chains, with goals that compromise the process from design to production and usage. This type of industrial-cultural colonialism has led to the degeneration in product design in general that we see today. As an example, let's take a look at a paradigm-shifting product, the laptop computer. Its basic design —the fold-down screen over a QWERTY keyboard—has become the quasi-standard around the world, even though the functionality and ergonomics of the design are compromised. Factories in Taiwan and China churn out laptops for prices that no one could have imagined ten years ago, populating the consumer electronics world with this flawed design.

Recently, there was a great opportunity to reverse this trend, by creating a fresh concept for the design of laptop computers for (and with) the children of the world—poor children who hadn't yet developed an idea of what a laptop should look like or how it should feel and function. I'm talking about Nicholas Negroponte's grand vision of the One Laptop per Child (OLPC) project's XO laptop, also known as the "$100 computer," in which I had some minor involvement. It was a noble effort but, sadly, it fell victim to cultural colonialism. Instead of taking innovation beyond the computer's technology and co-designing with the laptop's potential customers—most of whom were governments of populous countries such as China, India, and Brazil—Nicholas Negroponte and his team masterminded every angle of the project. As a result, they ignored some very inspiring and challenging input from their potential customers.

I remember an all-day meeting at MIT with a high-profile team from Brazil. The team came prepared with a number of concepts, and among them was the idea of producing the XO in Brazil—which would have had very real potential benefits for their country. But the idea didn't fly, because OLPC was unwilling to give up control. Maybe they thought they were emulating Steve Jobs in that regard, but if so, they had forgotten one very important fact about Steve: He actually listens. Slowly, the Brazilians started shaking their heads as they realized that OLPC wasn't thinking of a true joint venture (with joint benefits), and eventually the opportunity with Brazil faded. Soon thereafter, talks between OLPC, India, and China also came to a halt.

Ultimately, the "Western-designed" XO went into the supply chain for cheap laptops. Even a competent ODM from Taiwan couldn't correct the blandness of the design. The XO's price nearly doubled because the initial cost estimates were based on component costs alone, and the OLPC team never considered design alternatives that could have cut costs. Nor did they take advantage of the MIT students at their disposal who might have brought something new and fresh and daring to the design process. At the risk of sounding cynical, this experience illustrated cultural ignorance at work. If OLPC had bothered to find out what young students around the world really wanted and needed in a laptop, their research would have resulted in more innovative and culturally adequate solutions—and the project could have been successful.

Instead, the XO laptop ended up being a bland product that was about as "stylish" as a toy computer from Fisher-Price. Regular laptops are ergonomic disasters, and the XO's reduced size merely exacerbated the design's problems. When Intel presented its "Classmate" laptop and Asus launched the Eee mini-laptop (actually a very smart product), the XO computer found itself languishing within an even *more* crowded marketplace. Eventually, what began as a great idea with almost limitless industry-changing potential was reduced to one of those gadgets that will spend most of its product life on a closet shelf, before being chucked in a landfill.

The kind of research needed to design a product like the XO has to originate at various local levels, but it has to apply on a global level as well if we truly want to overcome the limitations of industrial-cultural colonialism. We should remember Marshal McLuhan's famous quote "think global, act local," but when we're looking at trend-setting areas in youth and urban fashion, sports, digital media, and entertainment, we also have to "think tribal, then go global." In this context, "tribal" can mean the style of a bling-bling brand like Phat Farm, a gladiator sports franchise like the National Football League, or cult brands like Burton snowboards and fashion, which have defined themselves through anti-establishment strategies that reject most of the classic ideas of branding. Even Hollywood is experiencing the competition of global tribalism. India has become a strong player in films, and its digital design industry is supported by open source distribution platforms, making it a truly globalized business.

Just as industrial-cultural colonialism has been a no-win strategy for everyone involved, ending it offers all of us a world of new opportunities. Those opportunities are perhaps most immediately rewarding for designers. By engaging in respectful collaboration with our international partners, we're able to experience each other's cultural richness and to use our new understanding to create better product concepts and better processes. And, as we work to design more environmentally responsible products, we'll be joining a worldwide effort aimed at spreading broad and lasting benefits throughout our global "tribe."

Shaping Consumer Behavior

All of this points to a fundamental truth that we *must* accept if we're going to promote ecological behaviors: We are not alone in this world. While promoting a widespread "we" mentality versus a "me" mentality might seem like a difficult undertaking (considering our seemingly bottomless belief in the creaky ideal of rugged individualism), there are examples everywhere that light the way. Some of them are in the form of public programs, but many others are private, for-profit, money-making ventures.

Driving is among our most cherished "lone wolf" behaviors in this country, and therefore offers some of the greatest challenge—and potential—for pursuing more environmentally responsible consumer behavior. In the morning and late afternoon rush hours, nearly every driver on the Bay Area freeways is alone in the car. It isn't the vast freedom of the road that calls these people. In fact, most of their commuting time involves little real driving. Instead, it's an extended stop-and-go crawl that breeds anger and resentment among drivers, even as it dirties the air with automobile exhaust. And yet, right beside these jam-packed, pollution-laced traffic lanes is a solution that is growing in popularity and use—the HOV (high occupancy vehicle) lanes. These lanes work well—after lots of research, the Metropolitan Transit Authority of Harris County, Houston, Texas, discovered that its HOV network is so efficient that it would take as many as twenty-four freeway lanes combined to service in individual vehicles the number of rush-hour passengers who carpool. This is an idea that works on a social and environmental level, so I can only wonder why even more people aren't using it.

Another very practical idea that still hasn't reached its full potential is car sharing, in which cars—not riders—are pooled for a more cost-efficient driving model. When you commute for work into San Francisco on a daily basis, owning and driving a car is a very painful and expensive proposition. Parking for two hours might cost you $18, and an all-day parking spot might run as much as $40—if you can find one. With car sharing, you pay an hourly usage rate (about $5 an hour) for your commuting vehicle. So, for example, you might pick up your car in the morning near your home in the East Bay, drive it into San Francisco, and drop it off for the next user. After work, you pick up another car, drive it home to Berkeley and drop it off for someone else to use there. You don't pay for parking or insurance, you don't pay for the privilege of keeping a car in your driveway or garage all evening, and you're less prone to make non-essential trips in an automobile. This idea makes good sense, and it's growing in popularity.

Public transportation is, of course, another solution to the "we versus me" dilemma. The American public transportation system pales in comparison to those in Europe or Japan, but the nation seems to be showing a renewed commitment to improving its infrastructure, with plans to expand and improve its public transportation network. That will take money, of course, but it was money—and robber baron capitalism—that gutted America's public transportation system in the first place. In the early 1900s, General Motors' long-time president, Alfred P. Sloan, Jr., began implementing a plan to expand auto sales and maximize profits by eliminating streetcars. In 1922, Sloan established a special unit within GM that was charged with, among other things, the task of replacing the United States' electric railways with cars, trucks, and buses. Consumers who no longer had the option of taking the streetcar turned first to the bus lines and, eventually, to owning and driving their own automobiles. GM's business strategy certainly did help change consumer behavior—just not for the better.

Today, thanks to the Internet and the vast growth of personal communications and social networking options, it's much more difficult for individual industries, let alone corporations, to control and manipulate consumers through disinformation or false promises. With the vast popularity of sites such as MySpace, Facebook, Second Life, or YouTube and consumer-tech/gadget blogs like Boing Boing or Gizmodo, the power of credibility and influence has shifted away from the mainstream content providers and toward more personal—and potentially polarizing—sources. These sites offer potential to any business or industry seeking an immediate connection to consumer thought and opinion. Outside-the-box entrepreneurs recognize the power and impact of a younger, far more engaged audience, so it was no surprise when Rupert Murdoch acquired MySpace and Google bought YouTube, even with the major copyright issues that surround those ventures.

We designers and business innovators can tap into this powerful new market, as well, and there's no stronger way to do that than by actively and publicly pursuing creative green strategies. People are listening and watching manufacturers more closely now than at any time in recent history. This gives us the opportunity to do the right thing for our companies and our consumers. By promoting green business agendas, we can join the growing movement to help continue to shape consumer behavior in ways that will be profitable for our organizations and for the world's environment.

○ triggering a holistic "reboot"

When we look at all professional fields that have considered or are considering green design, we find a lot of good ideas, concepts, and practical steps already being taken. What seems to remain in short supply, however, are holistic approaches to the problems we face, especially in the very challenging area of highly automated production and the sequential areas of usage and recycling. Beyond re-energizing our leadership, we need to reintegrate discrete expert fields into a more coordinated and integrated research effort.

By exploring what we *can* do, we can invent what we *need* to do. And the effort will most certainly have to integrate technology and business strategy, since any future business will be valued not only by the profits it earns, but also by the methods with which it achieves them. By the same token, technologists and scientists cannot rely only on technical parameters, but also must focus on the human impact of their projects. My proposals in this chapter may sound idealistic and "blue sky," but we need crazy, out-of-the-box, imaginative thinking if we want to keep our skies blue.

Since we've finally reached the point at which the environment is in visible decline because of our actions, and because we finally know that minor ecological "tweaks" and reductions won't save us from catastrophic events, those of us close to business, technology, and science don't have any other choice. We have to promote education on the issues (this is paramount for the monumental change at hand). But we also have to start offering better solutions right away—solutions that will convince the majority of customers to discard the old guard's offerings and support new ideas based on sustainable principles. Money makes the world go round, but we can—and must—choose leaders who know that "green" not "greed" is the winning solution.

As we stand on the edge of the future looking for the best way forward, it may be helpful to look back to the beginning of the industrial revolution and the thinking and writing of Adam Smith, the 18th century Scottish philosopher and pioneering political economist who wrote *The Wealth of Nations*. Although Smith had a profound influence on Western economic thinking, it is his book on ethics and human nature, *The Theory of Moral Sentiments* (1759), that I find more relevant today as we take on the challenge of dematerializing industry and business. Contrary to his later work, in which he ascribes social progress to economics, in *Moral Sentiments* Smith talks about emotions as the binding force in societies. His words offer an exercise in understanding and empathy:

> *How selfish so-ever man may be supposed, there are evidently some principles in his nature, which interest him in the fortune of others, and render their happiness necessary to him, though he derives nothing from it except the pleasure of seeing it.*

I urge everyone to read Smith's books—which remain as relevant today as on the day they were penned—and to remember his philosophy. It will come in handy for all of us, as we tackle what might be the greatest challenge of our lifetimes, that of saving our future by envisioning a new ecology of human culture driven by a green consciousness.

design-driven strategies for better business— and a better world

"In a consumer society, there are inevitably two kinds of slaves: the prisoners of addiction and the prisoners of envy."
—IVAN ILLICH

We're at a revolutionary moment in our approach to government, business, and economic growth. But, as we've seen, pulling off a successful revolution will require that we address a wide range of challenges. To adapt our system so that it helps ensure a good quality of life for everyone, we have to motivate the leaders of finance, big business, and politics to act for our common interest, rather than for special interests or the excessive benefits of themselves and a very few. And to do that, all of these leaders will need to work in concert with each other in a truly holistic way. Industrial nations will also have to kick the energy habit. We're consuming more and we're producing more, and that means we're polluting more. Although we need to produce cleaner energy, we need to focus even more on saving energy. To reduce the major causes of energy waste, we have to rethink the way we live, work, and consume— and do business.

That's a big order, but it also represents a defining moment for us all. Greening our industry is a unique opportunity for those of us who want to use our talents to help save the world and are willing to invest ourselves in the hard work of that mission. We have reached a stage in our world's history at which doing the best thing for the environment is tantamount to doing the best thing for our businesses. That balance of personal and worldly rewards makes the greening of industry a scalable movement, and one whose success is almost inevitable. As in nature, the entities that adapt and learn to thrive in the new economic environment will flourish, and the rest will die off.

As we've seen throughout this book, "change" is the mantra for businesses that want to keep pace with rapidly evolving cultures and consumer demands. But much of that change inevitably results in waste. Today, consumer technology products and the ways we use them change more rapidly than haute couture fashions. But it takes a lot more time, money, and manpower to retool for new industrial production than it does to shift to a new dress pattern—and it generates a lot more waste.

As a designer, I find it quite frustrating to see fully functional products discarded because they lack some incremental update in features or conformation, but the rapid advancement of technology makes this outcome inevitable. Newer—and often cheaper—technology turns products obsolete at a faster clip than ever before, and it doesn't help that components in fusion products like computers, cameras, displays, keyboards or touchpads, batteries, and antennas have non-synchronous lifecycles. This problem isn't limited to mobile phones and other small electronics, either. Washing machines with defective user interfaces, digital cameras with broken displays, or laptops with slow processors can't be fixed or upgraded, and so, into the landfill they go.

In this chapter, I want to take a closer look at some of the things that designers and executive leadership can do—and in some cases are doing right now—to address these issues and embrace green initiatives in their strategic business plans. By shedding old ways of thinking and operation, businesses can build and implement innovative strategies for success in the new, creative economy. The concepts I address here—fusion products, open-source design, and co-design within social networks—offer huge

WEGA SYSTEM 3000

My partners and I were working out of a rented
garage when Dieter Motte, owner and CEO of
Wega, hired our fledgling firm. Introduced in 1971,
our design for the System 3000 transformed
Motte's small company into a major brand

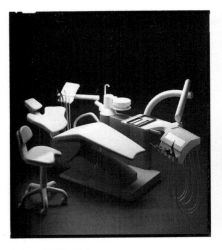

KaVo ESTETICA

Launched in 1972, our design for KaVo's "ESTETICA 1040" system improved the dental treatment experience for doctors and patients, and became the industry standard for the next twenty years.

LOUIS VUITTON

Louis Vuitton's signature prints go everywhere, with everything. Developed with frog design in the late 1970s, this affordable luxury strategy dramatically strengthened the LV brand's marketplace position.

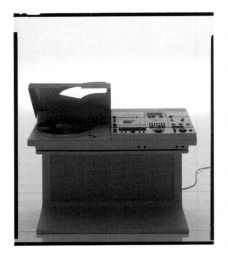

SONY-WEGA CONCEPT 51 K

In 1976, frog's design for the Wega Concept 51 Home stereo was stylish, compact, and easy to use—a perfect solution for that era. Today, the design is in the collection of the Museum of Modern Art, New York.

DISNEY CONSUMER ELECTRONICS

When frog licensed the Disney brand for consumer electronics in 2001, we co-designed directly with retailers such as Target and BestBuy. The product line's revenues skyrocketed.

SONY TRINITRON

In 1968, the Sony Trinitron's cathode ray tube offered the best picture in the industry, but its curved screen needed protection. frog's ground-breaking "black box" design answered that need and ushered out the "wood grain and brass" tradition in home entertainment systems.

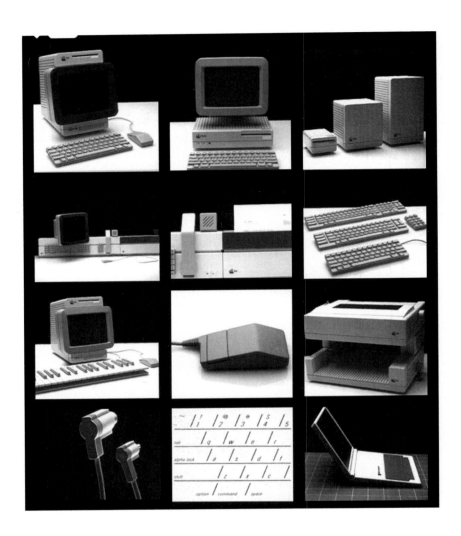

APPLE's BRAND and DESIGN DNA

frog collaborated on Apple's "Snow-White" design
language in the early 1980s. We worked closely
with Steve Jobs and Apple's developers to innovate
computer usability and appearance, resulting in
iconic products with no historic precedent.

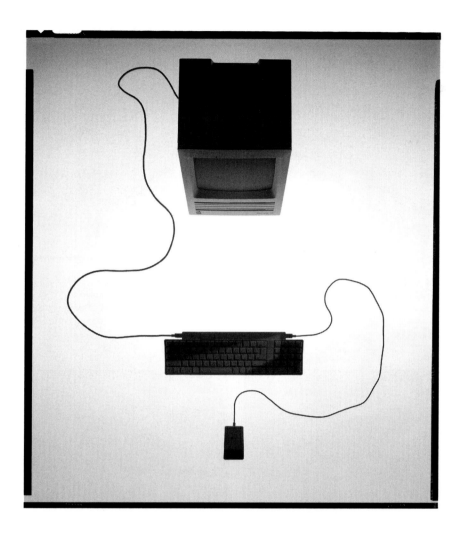

APPLE MACINTOSH SE

The release of the Apple IIc and the Macintosh
SE in 1984 established the role of design as a
key driver for business strategy. Apple's user
interface and media content humanized computer
technology – and helped to create a new culture

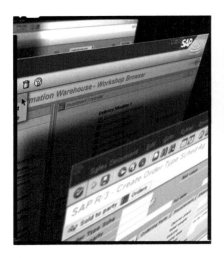

SAP R/3 and SAP PORTALS

In 1998, frog "humanized" SAP's R/3 enterprise software. We designed a more colorful and easier-to use interface and streamlined the software's speed and performance.

ALLTEL: "CELLTOP"

frog's design for Alltel's handheld communication portal offers a streamlined, intuitive connection to people, information, and entertainment.

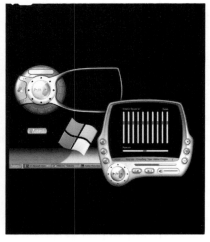

DISNEY CRUISE LINES

frog's retro-futuristic designs for the Disney Magic® and Disney Wonder® combine classic maritime elegance with starship swagger—and appeal to parents and children, alike.

MICROSOFT WINDOWS XP

In 2001, frog took part in the development of a more powerful and flexible Microsoft Media player system. We also updated the brand's image with a redesigned Windows logo.

LUFTHANSA AIRLINES

In the 1990s, Lufthansa's Executive Board asked frog to
create a new and more emotionally engaging image for
the airline and its base at the Frankfurt am Main Airport.
From check-in gates to plane interiors, our designs
helped redefine the modern air travel experience.

FUTURE PRODUCTS: "SMART ROBOTICS"

Networked robots will open new frontiers for services, civic engineering, living and working environments and extend human capabilities. *University of Applied Arts, Vienna (ID2 Master Class Esslinger): Lukas Dönz, Harald Tremmel, Dominik Premauer, Joachim Kornauth.*

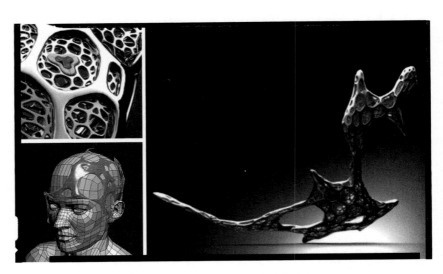

BITS, ATOMS, NEURONS & GENES: "BRAIN ENHANCER"

Scientific advances are challenging what "human" means, but design will make them relevant and determine what they can become. Bionic extensions of human functions will optimize the human experience. *University of Applied Arts, Vienna (ID2 Master Class Esslinger): Ewald Neuhofer.*

potential for improving the global viability and environmental sustainability of industrial products. And each of them can help form the core of design-driven strategies that just about any business can use to help firmly establish a foothold in the new and evolving creative economy.

○ fusion products: simple, flexible, sustainable

During our career at frog, my wife Patricia and I tried to launch an "outside-the-box" venture that failed, even as it taught us a lot in the process (a benefit that's easier to grasp now that we've survived the experience). And one of the most important lessons I drew from the experience had to do with the potential of fusion products—products that incorporate a variety of technologies in one package that serves multiple purposes.

In 1987, we started a new company called frox (as in "frog electronics"), with the goal of designing, developing, and producing a fully digital multimedia entertainment system. It was a truly visionary concept that just didn't pan out. Essentially, we wanted to integrate video-audio entertainment and computing into one system that would apply fully digital processing to all signals and data streams. Compared to our now decades-old concept, today's "media centers" are still well behind the curve.

For two years, the venture consumed most of our attention and energy, until we realized that neither the company nor the market was ready for the concept. What failed us in this undertaking wasn't the raw-force/pure-play technology we were developing. Instead, we were undone by human failure—in both the overly "corporate" management team who over-politicized the venture and overspent its funding, and the investors who didn't fully understand the painful process of applying high-tech capabilities to a consumer-focused product. Interestingly, after Patricia and I left the venture, the investors continued frox with a new management team and new money. They succeeded at launching the prototype, but it ultimately failed because it was too expensive and unreliable.

That doesn't mean that the need for convergent or "fusion" technologies has diminished. In fact, that need is greater than ever today. When we look at the consumer products that crowd our world, it doesn't take much to realize that many of them are based on the same technologies. Unfortunately, many of them also apply the same technologies multiple times in the same product. That kind of technological redundancy is wasteful, overly complex, environmentally unsound, and—in most cases—totally unnecessary.

As an example, let's consider the central processing unit or CPU. I have a CPU in the computer I'm using to write this book, as well as in my iPhone, my BlackBerry, my camera, my watch, my car, my stereo system, my iPod, my synthesizers, my washer, my dryer, and my television. But the redundant technologies of those devices go beyond the CPU. All of these products also have a display, a battery, a power supply, and some type of physical user interface. Each of those CPUs, interfaces, and so on is individually manufactured for each product, and therefore represents an expense for both the consumer and the manufacturer. Money that could have been spent on developing and manufacturing a better product—one that's more efficient, more powerful, more flexible, more enjoyable to use, more recyclable, and so on—has instead gone into reproducing the same technologies multiple times within mediocre products that have bad functionality. To trim this particular sort of waste and, at the same time, promote improved consumer products with the potential for widespread market success, we designers need to focus on creating fusion products.

We've already seen the development and broad consumer success of some notable examples of fusion products. Chief among these is the mobile phone. Back in the 1990s, most mobile phones offered users a computer, solid-state storage, a display, and a user interface in a pocket-sized package. The component missing from this mix was an optical system, but it didn't stay missing for long. Today, the camera-phone is ubiquitous, most offering both still and video image capture.

Another fusion product that has proven to be extremely useful—and some say even addictive—is the RIM BlackBerry. As an extremely mobile person who does a lot of global travel and business, my BlackBerry is one of my most productive and time-saving tools. Phone, email/text messaging, organizer, image-capture, media player, broadband Internet access and browser—there aren't many business functions I can't manage with this fusion tool. I also like its GPS function, and so does the rest of the world—location-based services are one of the hottest growth areas in wireless business.

In 2007, Apple introduced another level of "convergent fusion" with its iPhone. The iPhone also offers iPod music and video, and it brings full-featured Internet applications from the worldwide web to the palm of my hand. In addition to some very smart and directly integrated online services such as global weather, stock-tracking widgets, and more, the iPhone also demonstrates the future of a small-surface user interface with its touch-screen. That said, Apple and a community of developers are working hard to expand the iPhone's professional abilities. The next wave of iPhone fusion technology will provide environmental and medical monitoring. frog developed an experimental "green phone" that could, for example, check the bacteria levels of raw chicken in a grocery store, scan a barcode to track a product's environmental impact, and accept a battery recharge from a built-in hand crank.

Communication devices have made great strides as fusion products, but they aren't alone in their potential for leveraging fusion technologies. Automobiles offer another huge opportunity for fusion "makeovers." Electronic and digital components already represent a large segment of the manufacturing costs for modern automobiles, so it makes sense for us to start thinking about the car as a computer on wheels. Still, current technologies function in most automobiles as separate components. Even though driving, communications, navigation, and infotainment functions employ nearly identical technologies, they're all still constructed as independent components. If we look at the console of most cars—even those offering what most consider to be state-of-the-art design and technology—we find modern technology mired in past traditions.

In a BMW, for example, the instruments and controls are directly in front of the driver, but the iDrive controls are on the center console, in the space traditionally reserved for the car radio. The layout forces the driver to monitor two systems in two different locations and interact with them in two different ways. Further, the iDrive is so complex that even simple problems—say, a dead battery—require a trip to the BMW service center to have the car's computer rebooted. Bundling redundant technologies in single systems makes those systems more difficult to use, monitor, manage, and repair. In some cases, that difficulty represents a distraction that could even be dangerous.

I have an idea for a better way to design automotive electronics—and it offers a model for any designer seeking to develop useful fusion products. I believe that manufacturers should examine all of the ways that their automobiles could be driven and used safely and then integrate all the technologies necessary to support those uses in such ways that they work for the benefit of the driver, while avoiding wasteful production practices and excessive operating and maintenance costs (all of which would improve the car's sustainability factor). As new technologies such as distance control, traffic management, and time-based pollution reduction become more available, the need for the fusion of multiple and parallel functions within automotive designs grows even larger. Advances in other consumer technologies drive the same need.

Many designers today are tackling the challenges of fusing technologies within the electronic-digital home to combine a number of product systems—telephone, television, radio and music systems, personal computers, home security systems, and heating and cooling controls. This is the dilemma Patricia and I tried to address twenty-some years ago with frox, so I have some understanding of what it takes to bring these systems together. Home-based systems offer a rich illustration of the challenges and technological-strategic "gaps" we must confront when designing fusion products, and they are worth a closer look. To keep things simple, I'm going to focus on the chasm between semi-digital television and digital computing.

The issues plaguing the convergence of television technologies begin with the variety of incompatible signal standards in use around the world. The United States, Canada, and Japan (along with a few other Asian countries), still use an analog-based standard of transmitting and displaying video images called NTSC (National Television Standards Committee). Most of Western Europe uses the PAL (phase alternate line) system.

France, Russia, and parts of Eastern Europe adopted the more complex and less-robust SECAM (sequential color with memory) system, but many of those areas slowly are converting to PAL.

This technological melange is complicated by the fact that production studios have started recording in digital formats like 4:2:2—bandwidths way too "heavy" for broadcasting via antennas, cable, or satellites. To adjust to that limitation, we now have DTV (digital television), in which video and audio content is broadcast by a series of "discrete" signals, rather than in the one-piece signals used by analog television. DTV is more flexible than analog, and the picture is more stable, but DTV's pixels offer limited image resolution and the relatively crude audio scan rate makes music sound "metallic." The fact that most providers still use outdated broadcasting infrastructure only adds to DTV's shortcomings. The technology does carry one big advantage, however: It makes it possible to surf the Internet on your TV.

And that advantage would seem to make it possible to incorporate computers in DTV sets as fully digital devices—but it's not that simple. Television's legacy began in the living room, whereas computers found their first foothold in the office. Until operating systems (Windows/Vista, Mac OS, Linux, and so on) stop being office-centric technologies, their functions can't meld successfully with that of home entertainment devices. My eight-year-old grandchild, Lisa, gave me an interesting insight into this problem not long ago when she brought home a computer she designed and built at her Waldorfschule. She had built it from pre-cut pieces of plywood and had attached a number of fold-over "screen" images that she could flip through like the pages of a calendar. She started showing me her project by flipping its "display" to a very nice picture of the Windows opening screen (including the frog-designed Windows logo), but then she stopped. I asked her what the problem was—I thought maybe she wasn't sure whether her designer grandpa would like the next picture screen. But she just said, "Opa, the computer takes two minutes to start up."

Like I said, office computers aren't made for the living room. Few of us would be willing to wait as long for our television image to appear as we do for our computers to boot up. At the same time, there's no question that computers are becoming one of the world's foremost entertainment delivery mechanisms—just look at the incredible number of video clips viewed on YouTube. But computer technology isn't quite ready to displace the television entirely.

A true fusion home entertainment/computing products would also require a simple and practical user interface, something currently lacking in both televisions and office computers. People who don't regularly work with office-based computer systems and "productivity" software often have trouble understanding their incredibly complex user interfaces. Let's face it—feature-mania doesn't make computers fun to use. And what about that growing collection of remote controls in most living rooms? Few consumer devices are as unusable as most common remote controls, in spite of the vast resources invested in "designing," manufacturing, shipping, and disposing of them. And even more maddeningly complex and annoying is the "universal remote"—an ill-conceived and poorly implemented attempt at creating a fusion-type control for a variety of devices— TV, HiFi, DVD, CD player, VCR, and set-top box. Due to the multiple technologies (and redundant versions of the same technologies) these interface devices are "designed" to control, the only thing "universal" about them is the problems they offer the average user.

That brings us to the enigmatic device that links televisions to their digital content providers: the set-top box. Even though frog designed probably the nicest and easiest-to-use set-top box for SKY TV in 2006, the core concept behind these devices involves a technological quagmire, complicated even further by products like TiVo, Apple TV, and "media centers" from companies such as HP. In my opinion, the lack of "fusion" in all of these products is a result of short-sighted market opportunism. Companies always seem to want to grab for the low-hanging fruit, rather than stretching for something better.

Just imagine what kind of success a company might achieve by creating a fusion of music, radio, television, communication, infotainment, and personal-based productivity, all seamlessly connected with wireless full-media devices. It can be done, and it should be done. Forget the often-cited problem of the difference in user/device distances in the office (three feet) and the living room (ten feet). It's easy to design a wireless feature into a media-phone or a remote control that changes the character, sizes, and design paradigm of a user interface depending on the distance from the screen. With that device, users could adjust the display for close, detailed work, or long-distance infotainment.

A simple "magic wand" is possible. Andy Hertzfeld, Jaron Lanier, and I created one in 1989—the frox hypermedia system I described earlier. The fact that TVs aren't computers (despite running on computer technology) and computers aren't TVs (despite being able to display all kinds of media content) is more likely the result of unimaginative business models than anything else. Companies can become locked in their own frozen thinking patterns, and that chokes out the possibilities for growth through innovation and strategic creativity. And, in many cases, money isn't the problem. Consider for a moment how much money the world's major computer and entertainment companies have at their disposal.

Not only is the fusion of home entertainment and computing possible, but making it widely available would create a new market in which people would pay for better experiences that deliver more functionality and exhaust fewer resources. (They also won't have to wait, like my grandchild Lisa, for their computer to go through a two-minute boot cycle.) So, while many companies are already benefiting from the development and sale of fusion products, many more opportunities exist for taking advantage of this environmentally (and user-) friendly strategy.

○ open-source design: professional collaboration on a global scale

Designers and business leaders who are interested in advancing the cause of an ecologically sustainable production model have to learn to collaborate effectively. Their interest in working toward a shared goal must trump any creative egotism. That idea might sound almost painfully obvious, but it represents a dramatic departure from today's standard design practice. And it describes a working model that I call *open-source design*.

You're probably most familiar with the term "open source" as it's applied to computer system designs such as the IBM PC or Linux operating system but, in its broadest sense, the term refers to any concept that benefits (and, in its development, benefits from) an entire community rather than a few individuals within it. Good examples of historic open-source projects include Europe's many cathedrals and the rice terraces of Japan. Most open-source projects are commercially successful because of the initial community effort invested in them.

In spite of the success of the open-source efforts in computer software and hardware, we haven't yet seen an open-source solution for holistic product development. In my view, we need to start such an initiative, because the ecological stakes of not doing so are too high. Only by sharing our best knowledge and combining our talents on a global scale can new products like the ultimate zero emission vehicle or the long-lifecycle digital device become reality.

How do we start? I believe that shared tools are the key to implementing open-source product development. Ivan Illich—the Austrian philosopher, educator, priest, and social critic—was quite influential in my own education. He describes this ancient concept of sharing and open collaboration in his book *Tools for a Convivial Society,* when he notes that the tools of communal collaboration (or conviviality, as he phrased it) "*. . .give each person who uses them the greatest opportunity to enrich the environment with the fruits of his or her vision.*"

Computer software (Linux) and hardware (chips) development have a strong history in open-source design. Back in the mid-1970s, Lee Felsenstein, an electronics designer involved in the Berkeley Free Speech movement, took the idea of communal living and community bulletin boards from the 1960s U.S. counterculture and applied it to computer design. His goal was to design and build new computers through a collective effort, made possible by connecting individual hobbyists all over the country. By doing so, he hoped to bring together groups of people who knew and understood every detail of the systems they were running, including maintenance and repair. With Felsenstein's idea providing "tools for conviviality," the whole design process for computers became a convivial process in itself.

Lee's first step toward his goal was to distribute the schematics for a computing machine as widely as he could throughout the then fledgling tech community, in order to gather its ideas for improving the machine's design. That collaboration resulted in the design for the "Tom Swift computer terminal." Then, in 1975, Lee and several of his fellow collaborators formed an organization in Silicon Valley called the Homebrew Computer Club, a loose-knit group of people trying to push the notion of cooperative computer design. There were about thirty people at the club's first meeting, but within a year, the group had grown to include almost six hundred members. The designs they came up with—even those for commercial products, including Steve Wozniak's first personal computer—were shared, discussed, and developed through ideas that fed upon each other.

After Apple became a huge start-up success, IBM embraced the concept of open-source development in its second foray into personal computing. The "IBM PC" wasn't an IBM product in the traditional sense: The processor was from Intel, the storage devices from Seagate and Shugart, the floppy-disk drives from Asian manufacturers, and the software operating system from a small start-up company called Microsoft. In fact, the entire business model represented a radical departure in strategy. In a November 1984 article in *Creative Computing,* P.D. Estridge, IBM's "father of the PC," described his strategy as follows:

> *"It is choice that is the underpinning of IBM's commitment to open architecture: providing information and specifications which encourage others to develop options and programs that run on our systems. This approach has enabled hundreds of companies and individuals to develop hundreds of hardware peripherals and thousands of applications which people can choose for their IBM personal computers."*

Estridge understood the potential benefits of open-source collaboration, unlike those who see it largely as a potential threat to creative control and market dominance.

So how can we apply the benefits of open-source design and development to our efforts to promote a "less-is-better" culture within our industrial systems? First, we will have to set advanced standards that designers and developers all over the world can reference when creating concepts for singular components, sub-assemblies, or complete products. With an open-source framework for mobile phones, digital still and video cameras, handheld computers, media players, medical sensors, and environmental monitors, developer groups could focus their collaborations on creating the best possible display, or finding the most efficient energy sources, or combining components into new applications—such as environmentally sustainable mobile phones.

Open-source design will be a big departure from today's "insular" and brand-exclusive approach, because it will establish a system for defining identity and rewards through concept-driven innovations and choices. Most product groups today look like collections of clones, anyway, so open-source design would actually raise the level of creative quality in most industries. Like working with LEGO® blocks, designers could choose from among various design elements that share similar connecting features to create something totally unique. The open-source system would generate savings in tools, materials, and recycling in multiple stages of the product lifecycle, because it would enable designers and manufacturers to draw from a set of established components (displays, keyboards, enclosures, and user interfaces). These products would enjoy a greatly increased period of use as well. Outdated or broken components could be easily replaced, rather than triggering the disposal of the entire product (most wireless device components have relatively long lifecycles).

By that standard alone, the open-design concept will change the way we view the products we create. Instead of today's "disposable" mentality, designers will develop products designed for broader and more varied markets, because they will be able to collaborate with a much wider development group to design, customize, and upgrade devices. Open-source products can evolve continually, right along with the ways in which they're used. And, through the use of common components and technologies combined with broader user and developer input, open-source design and development would also contribute to the development of more—and better—fusion products.

From an industry point of view, an open-source strategy like the one I'm suggesting would reduce the material resources required for production, but it wouldn't necessarily reduce profits. Think about it: When a major ODM produces zillions of wireless devices at rather meager profit margins, the parent company is taking on massive risks associated with inventory and exchange rate volatility. Cutting revenues in half and doubling the absolute profits—which actually means quadrupling them—would be a great achievement for just about any global business. And that's just the kind of achievement we can realize through open-source design.

Open-source product development also would dramatically lower the barriers of entry for new product designs. Many companies—especially start-ups—waste incredible amounts of money just getting their physical product to the marketplace. In fact, that very reason has led many venture capitalists and other funding sources to label physical products as investment "negatives." VCs will fund ten software start-ups before they take on one new hardware project—which is a primary reason that our software gets better and better, while the hardware we use it in remains bland and generic. By lowering the barriers to new product entries, we would also enjoy a heretofore unheard of strategic benefit. Imagine: Before sinking any money into product development, design, or engineering, companies and their customers could "test drive" new products. A simple open-source circuit board with programmable chips sets could simulate (and emulate) nearly every imaginable device function.

And, as an added but very important benefit, this model could begin as a hybrid of open-source components and those that require specific approvals or life-critical functionality, such as medical, transportation, or aviation devices. As an example, let's look at glucose meters, which diabetics use to monitor their blood glucose levels (Flextronics designs and manufactures these meters for LifeScan, a company that retains frog's design service and was later acquired by Johnson & Johnson). These meters have a short needle that users inject into their fingertips to produce a drop of blood, which they then place on a measuring strip. A computerized sensor in the meter measures the blood's glucose count, then communicates its findings to the user via a small digital display. In addition to the simple readout, software programs designed for this system put the measurement into the context of time and the user's biorhythm.

Even though these glucose meters are rather complex products, they are sold at incredibly low prices. The manufacturer makes its money on the strips (a business model like that behind the old Kodak camera, where selling film was the company's real business and the cameras were merely "film eaters"). Unfortunately, the technology of these glucose meters is far from stellar—the devices require that users stab themselves, and that hurts. To address this shortcoming, an offshoot company of HP's medical business, called Pelikan Technologies, has worked with Flextronics to develop a new meter technology that is both elegant and humane. The technology enables the meter to extract blood from a patient's body without pain and to measure glucose levels directly without further procedures. But because Pelikan Technologies is a small start-up, it has to develop an entire product around its innovation before it can get funding. That's a huge waste of the company's resources *and* creative potential.

An open-source approach to building a better glucose meter would be to turn the task of development over to a community of engineers who have direct experience with diabetes (with roughly twenty-one million American diabetics there should be enough engineers for this task). They could collaborate with each other and choose the best components from each manufacturer, which they would combine for the best and most pain-free solution. Building new solutions around proven parts that have medical FDA approvals would be a better way to find the best design than today's "every company for itself" strategy.

So what's holding us back? We've already seen a major revolution in consumer behavior and Internet-enabled social networking, so making the step to open-source product development should be a natural evolution. These open-source networks could critique ideas, test-drive virtual proposals, and collaborate on new designs. And the products resulting from these collaborations would be better tailored to consumer needs, available at attractive prices, and held to a global ecological standard.

I believe that the open-source development model will take hold, and those designers and business leaders who are able to work with it will win in the new economy, while those who can't make the switch will lose. If you think I'm off-base here, think for a moment of past paradigm shifts in technology that have resulted in the demise of global brands and companies. Polaroid comes to my mind here—a company I actually worked with in the 1980s. They were so blinded by their inventive tradition and the money they made on their original breakthrough of "instant" self-developing film that they didn't realize the growing threat posed by digital imaging.

If we turn the clock back to 1990, Polaroid's biggest asset was a global user-base that bought the company's cameras but also—and more importantly—bought its film. On paper, Polaroid looked agile, with about $3 billion in revenues. Internally, however, the company was at odds with the vision of its founder and inventor, Dr. Edwin Land. Instead of developing the inventive and innovative thinking that brought so much success in the first place, Polaroid used much of its capital to defend itself against copycat technologies. The company refused to explore digital imaging, even as new start-ups out of MIT sprang up along Route 128 and on Kendall Square, offering a glimpse of the digital future. What killed Polaroid was its patent-centric mindset and its firm focus on the past, rather than the future. When the technology it defended so hard against competitors became obsolete, the company became obsolete.

But what if Polaroid had opened up instead of hunkering down? Just imagine if the designers among its loyal global user-base had collaborated on an open-source "image system" based on, but not limited by, the company's previous success. First of all, there would have been a different mindset within the company. Polaroid's brand and product experience was about instant images, not necessarily about cameras and instant film. An open-source strategy would have kept Polaroid on the path of "instant imaging" because, as the technology developed, the choices would have become more varied and flexible. Open-source collaborators would have tried many crazy things outside the typical Polaroid "box." Also, I'm sure that such a developer community would have created some early applications based on the emerging digital technologies of the time, including personal computers, networks, and content management. Polaroid would have become a much more environmentally responsible company as well, as it shifted away from paper-based images created with messy chemicals to material-free, viewer-based images and other technological innovations with a greatly reduced ecological load factor.

Most designers are individualists and can be territorial about their designs, but when I discussed the concept of open-source design with my students in Vienna, they enthusiastically responded to the idea. We decided to experiment with the idea, and we had a blast. One project recycled Olivetti's famous Valentine typewriter by Ettore Sottsass and Perry King and applied it to a futuristic concept of a portable computer. When Sottsass died during that semester, the team took the task even more seriously and created both a touching homage to Ettore and an extremely advanced computer. Everybody who sees it loves it and wants to have and use it—we may even find a company to bring it to market.

Building on this positive experience, I then dedicated an entire research semester to open-source design. My students proposed their own project ideas, which were followed by a discussion and a vote. I've seen a number of very interesting ideas come from these collaborations, including an "Air Helmet" for life in polluted areas, a mobile phone with modular hardware and software (the latter combining all the best features of Symbian, Apple, Google, Linux, and Microsoft), an "Emergency Rescue" robot, a portable meta-factory, a modular baby stroller, a "ZEV for a Nomadic Life," virtual traffic signs, a digital soccer pitch, a "Magic Flute" synthesizer, and an information system layered upon everyday objects called "Third Space."

Once a group of my students accepts an idea, we get to work creating it. Our working method is fundamentally different from the traditional model. We start by analyzing a similar product or technology, and then we use what we've learned as the starting point for our own design. The key principle is simple: Find what's good, make it better, and put it into a more meaningful and innovative context. The student teams also can take ideas from other teams and apply them to their own projects—this often happens when we're working in robotics and user interfaces. No one gets an individual grade on these projects, so the collective energy is amplified by synergy.

It's true that individual intellectual property rights stand in the way of open-source design. In fact, when I present the concept of open-source design, I'm frequently asked if it won't result in a marketplace choked with copycat products. This certainly could be an issue, but I think it's time that we recognize that many of today's products are, in some ways, outgrowths of other products. Again, the iPod serves as an interesting example. Apple applied Creative's digital music player software and made it a success—something Creative hadn't yet accomplished. Apple paid Creative $100 million for legal rights to its user interface, an arrangement that, in the end, benefited us all. We consumers got a perfect product and content solution from Apple, which in fact liberated the act of listening to music. Apple's iPhone continues this strategy of innovating by combining proven technologies and concepts in a new and meaningful way. And when you opened the calculator on the first iPhone, you saw an exact digital rendering of the user interface of Dieter Rams' Braun calculator from the 1960s (an interface that proves that sometimes we don't need "new," we just need "better").

A move toward open-source design might also help us step out of the shadow of the legal morass that surrounds patent law. Intellectual property rights have been one of the pillars of capitalism's success, but because of the abuse and the incompetence of legal systems, many companies don't even apply for patents anymore. When settling a lawsuit is cheaper than winning one, intellectual property laws and systems that promote litigation can pose a real threat to innovation—a threat that might be diminished through open-source design and development.

These are just some of the many issues that I believe are accelerating our transition toward a model of open-source design, product strategy, and product development. Not only is this transition possible, it's necessary. But to really make the most of open-source collaboration, we need to understand that a product's co-developer might also be that product's consumer. And that means that we can take collaboration one step further than the formal, professional model of open-source design to one of co-designing within social networks.

○ co-design through social networks: giving customers a say—and a stake

Product design is and will remain an elitist profession. Simply put, real design quality never will be a matter of democracy. But the Internet has changed something very essential about the ways in which people communicate and form relationships—and that includes the relationships of consumers and the products, technologies, and services they consume. Given these changes, I propose that designers and manufacturers should combine efforts to promote a concept of co-design that involves consumers and takes place within a social networking structure. I'll explain how this might work, but let's begin by looking at how the current consumer/manufacturer relationship has evolved.

In the old days, consumers were mere numbers to the businesses that fed off of them. Designers and manufacturers alike treated consumers as little more than statistical units that were useful for projecting sales or calculating profit margins. Marketing managers characterized consumers by their superficial preferences, giving them labels such as "emulators," "emulator achievers," "belongers," and "need-directeds." Even when marketers attempted to focus on "real people," they typically saw only their own manufactured versions of reality. In short, companies and their marketing teams have not always had the full, real picture of who their customers are and what they think.

Now, as digital tools and Web 2.0 shared-content solutions bridge space and time, people in very different places can connect, coalesce, and assert their group power as consumers to buy or reject new products and technologies. The Internet has eliminated the barriers of space and geography with MySpace and other social networks, where communities of people who share interests and activities can connect and communicate. Customers have gone from being marketing-manipulated "subjects" to becoming powerful partners in the economic process. That's why now is the time to integrate consumers into the design process—not as slaves to the designer's esthetic choices, but as a new vanguard that up-ends the whole notion of mass marketing.

Co-design isn't a new concept. In fact, it hues closely to the pragmatic American tradition of bringing together different people to draw upon the best of their ideas, views, and priorities to produce something that works for all, benefits all, and is designed by and for all. One could say the U.S. Constitution offers an early example of American-style co-design. Philosophically, co-design is based on Immanuel Kant's idea that, in order to arrive at a good solution, we have to draw upon reason—what Kant called *a priori* knowledge—rather than information stemming from our previous life experiences. Just about everything we do builds on something that's already there and already has a purpose.

To imagine how a co-design social network might function, think of it as a combination of an online social network and a digital eBay-style bazaar, with some collaborative Internet applications for product development thrown in. Using that model, we could create communities that would actually interact with companies on the development of products that meet their needs, wishes, ideas, and price range. All stakeholders would have a real interest in the process and its outcome. In the co-design model, customers and users—who aren't part of the typical design process today—would be included from the very beginning. In fact, the co-design process could be triggered by expert customers and users, who might ask for a product, service, or experience that no company had even considered. Companies, much more than customers, are fixated on the status quo.

This approach to product design has the potential for a huge economic and environmental impact. Instead of pushing a mass-produced product or a service to a more or less anonymous market, companies could invest their resources in creating something that has a pre-existing customer demand. Then customers could cut an economic deal. "This is what we need and want, and this is what you've said you can supply," they might say. "Now what will it cost, and when can we get it?" By more closely linking supply and demand, companies can eliminate economic and environmental waste—no rebate, no discount, no trashing of inventory.

The co-designed process should improve the quality of products as well. Designs based on target groups, focus tests, and user poll "samplings" inevitably result in mediocre products and middle-of-the-road solutions. The co-design process I'm proposing involves a dialogue in which groups of potential customers communicate their specific wishes to companies. Designers can then turn these wishes into concepts—hardware and/or software—which they then can refine in close collaboration with the customer group on one side and the ODMs on the other. Finally, a contract outlines the final concept, price, and timing, the orders and pre-payments come in, and the ODM develops and manufactures the product. The result will be, in essence, just what the customers ordered. Because it will enable businesses to cut most of the current overhead for administration and marcom (corporate-speak for marketing and communications), companies will find this working model financially attractive. Designers will enjoy this working model, too, because it will provide a personally rewarding working relationship with the public and a cultural richness our current approach to design doesn't offer.

Of course, one big question remains: How can we make co-design a reality? Before the Internet, this kind of collaboration could only take place on a local level. A historic example comes from 180 years ago, when the furniture manufacturers of Vienna designed chairs and tables in collaboration with coffee-house customers and an architect. I participated in a much more recent example, when I started to work with Sony in 1974. At that time, Sony had a microcosm of the co-design model with its customers in Tokyo and London. Even as we designed concepts specifically tailored to the tastes of individual cultures and locations, the vast geographical space that separated us from those locations remained a big limitation. But our CEO Akio Morita would tell us, "Our concept for the London market can achieve 2 percent market share. If we can achieve these numbers in one hundred global markets, we have a huge opportunity." And most of the time it worked.

Those geographic barriers have come down, and I believe that a qualified consumer commitment spread thinly around the globe is the future trend of social network-based co-design. Co-design will give companies pinpoint marketing and tailored production, as it reduces financial and material waste. And, equally important, this design model serves our global culture by being both more personal and more sustainable.

○ designing the new industrial revolution

The credo "What's good for business is good for the world" has changed somewhat. Now, if it isn't good for the world, it probably isn't going to be good for business either. Around the world, businesses are connecting the dots between improved environmental responsibility and increased economic sustainability. We've already seen the launch of initiatives aimed at promoting ecologically responsible decision making by large companies. The Dow Jones Sustainability Index, for example, provides information about the way corporations conduct their businesses. This kind of information has power. The index has prompted Apple to ask its ODMs to design and produce its products without poisons, mercury, or cyanic glues. But the Sustainability Index is just a first step—and in my opinion, a relatively benign one—toward raising awareness of the environmental impact of consumer products and experiences.

Ultimately, I believe that all products and processes will be priced and taxed according to how much or little they affect the environment (what I described in the previous chapter as the ecological load factor or ELF). As all of us become more conscious of the carbon footprints our technologies and lifestyles and consumer choices leave behind, we come face-to-face with the reality that our own health and welfare may be more closely linked with that of the earth than with the rise and fall of short-term market profitability.

Given the size of the challenges, no single discipline—even design—can single-handedly take on the task of "greening" industry and business. The industrial system is too complex, with too many different players. The cycle of production, usage, and recycling is finite, meaning nothing within it will just disappear. And we can't just discard established systems, such as our electric grid or transportation networks. Instead, we have to transform them organically, in stages. We've already looked at how egotism, special interests, and limited competencies among the world's leaders in business, science, politics, and industry have fractioned efforts toward environmental progress and limited progress with narrowly defined motivations and goals. Nevertheless, designers have a unique opportunity to drive the development of sustainable products by virtue of our role in the early stages of the product lifecycle process. But we can't do it alone.

Alix Rule, a student of politics at Oxford, underscored this point in her *In These Times* blog entry titled "The Revolution Will Not Be Designed." Rule noted that, in spite of the optimism expressed by designers, we need more than a "can-do attitude" to address "the nastier socioeconomic and environmental corollaries of growth." Like Rule, I admire the progressivism behind much of the current generation of design thinking. But I also know she's right when she says that the belief that design can save the world without a "coherent set of ideas" represents a type of progressivism that is "naïve, at best." Even if designers *could* save the world, we have to face the fact that many of them lack the knowledge and/or desire to create sustainable concepts for any effect other than a visually expressive statement. Environmentally driven design, at its core, is not about the "next new thing" but about "the next better thing," and many designers find this goal very boring and limiting. That's why designers rely on strong alliances with forward-thinking business leaders to devise sustainable strategies that will succeed in the world as it is, while helping to shape the world as we want it to be.

For all of these reasons, greening our industrial processes is going to require a much deeper understanding of our potential. The ideas I've outlined in this chapter all involve technologies or products or practices that are currently available or can be easily adapted from existing models, if we're willing to do the hard work of changing our attitudes and approaches to the way we do business. As we've seen, advancements such as these are critical elements for developing and achieving sustainable strategic business models that are driven by strategic innovation toward a more environmentally—and economically—sound future.

3

the factories

The center of power is in the factory.
—AKIO MORITA

I love factories! I've loved them since my childhood when I would go with my father to buy fabric at the weaving mills in Reutlingen, Germany, and when I toured the steel plants with my relatives in the Ruhrgebiet, and later, when I hung around the assembly lines at a Mercedes-Benz factory as an engineering intern at ITT. The efficient clatter of the machines, the teamwork of those controlling them, and the sheer breadth of the operations fascinated me.

That was over forty years ago, and though the factories of my youth were true wonders, today's industrial workshops are far more advanced. After four decades of working in the consumer product world, I've seen factories go from models of efficient manufacturing to the vanguard of modern technology—more sophisticated than any other high-profile technological achievement of the past half-century. We've explored designing and developing new creative business strategies that involve more environmentally sustainable products and practices, but the place where all of those ideas come to life is in the factory.

○ welcome to the machine

Most people—and certainly most professionals outside of manufacturing and supply chain management—don't understand factories as well as they should. These high-tech workshops play a key role in the industrial process and have become major drivers in the seismic shifts taking place in global business—in particular the shifts resulting from outsourcing. In fact, outsourcing has become so intricately intertwined with the manufacturing process that we cannot take a close look at one without considering the other.

Outsourcing has become a pariah among the working class, and for good reason. It almost always means local jobs are lost to cheaper labor abroad. That's because the practice has become a single-minded monetary decision for business executives who directly equate outsourcing with cheap labor and low cost. Any talk of outsourcing as a means to foster collaborative innovation is still just talk—the zillions of boring products on the market are proof enough of that. But, as I explain in this chapter, outsourcing can be a positive strategy—if the consumer technology industry is willing to take a different approach to it.

The current form of outsourcing has come to rule manufacturing because we've boxed ourselves into a single globally networked economy with most of its factories humming away in the East. If we want to break out of that box—and that's a growing movement in the Western world—designers and manufacturers have to adopt more integrated and collaborative processes so as to maximize the still-dormant potential in the global technology supply chain. And, I'm sorry, but all of those unimaginative, penny-pinching executives who have little or no manufacturing experience simply need to go. If we want to revitalize our industrial system, we need leaders and decision-makers who have a thorough understanding of how factories work.

Designers can help provide that leadership, but they, too, must have a firm grasp of factory operations. Product designs must be translatable into production runs of millions of units, and if we want to be able to advance and improve the manufacturing process, it's paramount that we understand every step of it. Too often, designers see limitations, rather than potential, in the factory. In fact, designers have a long history of viewing the factory as the enemy of true creativity. When bland projects are rejected by the market, designers blame the factory guys first. But, in reality, 99 percent of these "rejects" aren't viable product ideas—they're just half-baked realizations of the designer's vision of what a product *might* be.

The conceptual disconnects between designers and their manufacturing partners have limited their potential for convergence. The result is more and more generic "picture frame" designs that merely tweak the look of existing products, rather than truly improving their form or function. To break out of this monotonous mold, designers are going to have to step out of their studios and get some first-hand experience in the magic of today's factories. Then, perhaps, their designs can win a place in people's lives, not just in the glossy pages of style magazines.

I've always designed products in the closest possible collaboration with the hands-on manufacturers, whether those were factory people or software programmers, and I encourage other designers to do the same. When we fully understand the capabilities of the people and systems we're collaborating with, we can join forces with the "productioneers" and really push the envelope. And, by collaborating through every step of the design process, we can work to improve the manufacturing process, test new ideas, shorten the time-to-market, and reduce both costs and waste. We designers can't just demand that manufacturers do a great job turning out "our" products. We need to pitch in and help with the process. And believe me, today's factories are more than ready to do their part.

Almost all Western brand-name manufacturers have their goods produced on a contract basis at ODMs (original design manufacturers) in Asia or Eastern Europe, but most business leaders—and the designers who work with them—don't realize that these Asian ODMs are far more flexible than their Western counterparts. That flexibility represents a much more valuable commodity than mere cheap labor. These factories take on so many customers that their products often change on a daily basis, and their machines can be programmed on the fly. That kind of nimbleness offers designers a lot more creative potential, if they take the time to work side-by-side with ODMs and understand the technology they command.

Of course, globalization offers its own challenges for the consumer technology industry. Design and production processes are parceled out among various companies, and all of that outsourcing and cross-sourcing can seem frustratingly complex to most designers. Even tech-savvy executives can falter as they navigate this global maze. But if businesses in the consumer technology industry want to stay competitive, their designers and executives will have to step up to the plate. In the new and ever-evolving global economy, those who know how to engineer and manufacture will have an advantage over those who know how to brand and market products. So it's vital that all of us learn about (and learn to love) factories.

o the high costs of "cheap" production

If a Western company is going to work with an Asian-based factory, it's going to have to face the question of outsourcing. There are numerous ways to outsource, and people often confuse them, despite important differences. *Offshoring* is the transfer of an organizational function—a factory or a business unit—to another country. *Outsourcing* involves contracting with an outside supplier for services or materials, and that may or may not involve some degree of offshoring. Outsourcing conducted with more than one partner is called *multi-sourcing*—a practice that is actually quite common in the production of major IT projects. With the ongoing evolution of global collaboration, the differences between these working arrangements grow fuzzier, but it's still important that we understand them as we work to shape our own product lifecycle processes.

When a company moves a major part of its business to another country, as it does with offshoring, it risks alienating workers and—to a certain extent—compromising its social responsibility at home. In exchange for those risks, the company may reduce its costs through cheap labor, foreign government incentives, and relaxed legal and fiscal regulations. Back in the 1980s, Singapore structured its laws to attract foreign business. The plan worked. Philips relocated its consumer electronics unit to Singapore, Panasonic brought in a major audio business unit, and HP set up its printer and calculator unit there, as well. These and other newly relocated companies reduced their costs and became more competitive.

And then certain cracks in the business model began to show. HP had to bring a large number of "ex-pats" to Singapore, which actually cost much more than if it had kept these employees working back in the States. And the company grappled with the challenge of maintaining and advancing the "HP Way" within its new environment—which also cost more than planned. Eventually, HP outsourced its detailed design, manufacturing, and logistics for its most vital business division, its printers, to Flextronics. In fact, Flextronics acquired several offshore factories whose original owners couldn't manage well on foreign soil—a move that became an important strategic innovation to the offshoring business model.

HP's experience illustrates a reality that forms one of the key challenges of offshoring: What works well "at home" may not work at all overseas. The company's partnership with Flextronics is also a perfect example of how offshoring can morph into outsourcing—with even better results.

Many companies turn to outsourcing to save money or to bring specific competencies to the table, but outsourcing can also be an attempt to catch up to the marketplace. In 1983, Apple had no internal production knowledge, and outsourcing with competent partners like Sony, Samsung, and Canon helped the company turn out world-class products in a very short time. For outsourcing to result in that kind of success, however, it has to be a true partnership, in which a company transfers the management and day-to-day execution of an entire business function to its outsourcing provider.

Many business leaders and owners are loath to give away that kind of control, but do it anyway to advance their companies' financial goals. That's why outsourcing relationships often work best when they're carefully defined by specific contracts that outline performance objectives, not just payment milestones.

Outsourcing has always touched a nerve because of the perception that foreign companies are stealing local jobs. But many of those jobs have been driven overseas by executives, managers, and shareholders who are indifferent to or ignorant of both the pitfalls and the unique strategic opportunities of outsourcing. Very few leaders dare to think ahead, to try to imagine a strategy for long-term success, by building valuable assets with vertically integrated processes, innovation, and an admirable and defendable culture (all of which add value). Instead, many run for the cheapest shop abroad, and when they do Wall Street applauds—at least it did, back when the "numbers" still looked good. But today, a growing number of consumers and manufacturers alike understand that the absurdly low price points of some goods from overseas often require brutal working conditions along with shortcuts on quality and safety. The latest recalls from toys to medication manufactured in China have shown the ugly face of this process, and both sides of the outsourcing relationship are paying dearly.

Farsighted business leaders develop a broader and more detailed understanding of both the benefits and costs of establishing strong outsourcing relationships (I call these arrangements "smart sourcing," and I talk about that later in the chapter). They also realize that some of those costs aren't just one-time transactions, but represent unending losses. Businesses (and societies) suffer a number of losses that can threaten their core identity when outsourcing relationships aren't well designed or well managed, and these losses are worth looking at in some detail.

Lost Product Knowledge

Outsourcing may seem like a recent industrial phenomenon, but my first encounter with it was in 1966, when I was an engineering intern with the quality-control department in ITT's German consumer-electronics company Schaub-Lorenz/Graetz. Our German designs for portable radios— back then, the rage with young people—were of very high quality. But, with prices ranging from 100 to 190 Deutschmarks (at the time, the U.S. dollar was worth about three Deutschmarks), they were a bit too expensive to become big sellers. Just before I joined ITT, its executives had come up with the idea to launch a low-cost brand called "Oceanic," which could be sold at retail for 29 to 99 Deutschmarks. To hit that low price point, the radios would be designed and engineered by ITT's European engineers and "stylists," but manufactured by the Japanese companies Sanyo and Silver. About six months later, we received the first pilot-run production for testing. Our Japanese partners had reduced the number of required parts for the radio dramatically, and its sound and quality ratio still were within acceptable ranges.

But disaster struck with the first real deliveries. The products failed to meet the minimum quality ratio of one failure per 10,000 units. Sending the products back wasn't an option. Shipping between Japan and Europe at that time took about six weeks. This meant that *every unit* had to be hand-checked, and faulty parts had to be replaced. We had to open the housing, take out the board, clip out a faulty diode, and then manually solder in a new one (this experience taught me a lot about electronic board work). After re-testing the unit, we had to put the whole thing back together again and slip it into its packaging in such a way that consumers wouldn't notice it had ever been out. This process added about ten Deutschmarks to the cost of each unit, which would have translated into about 35 Deutschmarks at retail.

Then came "stage two" of ITT's losses in this venture. After about two years, Sanyo and Silver had learned the lessons of how to manufacture electronics for European markets and began producing superior products— at which point they launched their own electronic products in the European market, including high-performance radios. Their radios resembled ITT's in both electronics and visual design, but they cost about 30 percent less than ours. In the end, ITT sold off its consumer-electronics business unit altogether, which meant that many competent engineers and workers lost their jobs—which especially hurt the communities in Pforzheim and Bochum, where the factories were shut down.

As I stated earlier, outsourcing requires transferring know-how, not just work. And when organizations farm out their manufacturing functions, they can end up starving out their native product knowledge and skills. Designers and engineers flourish when asked to answer human challenges, advance culture, and inspire the marketplace, but they *need* the factory and its support system for nutrition. I have seen truly great engineering and design teams lose their professional edge within three to five product generations after their companies started to outsource. Today's high-tech products have a life cycle of about nine to eighteen months, so this fall from excellence can happen in less than three years. The power is with the factories, and that's exactly where we have to focus our efforts on creating a smarter, more environmental supply chain strategy.

Lost Manufacturing Skills

Today, some of the most brilliant production facilities in human history—equipped with the latest state-of-the-art German and Japanese production technology—are located in China. Over the past few years I've been shocked to realize how the vast capabilities of these factories are being wasted by Western companies that use them to manufacture primitive products with shamefully bland designs and painfully repetitive technology. In essence, we have reached a crucial point in industrial history: Taiwan and China have outpaced us in their knowledge of production and supply-chain engineering. Product design and engineering may soon follow.

That's why we need to convince more executives and professionals to develop a deep love and understanding of manufacturing. We need engineers, designers, and product managers to spend real time working within factories. In fact, that was the original HP Way. Engineers and designers worked directly in the factory, separated from the assembly lines only by glass walls. I remember an HP complex in which the engineers' glass-walled enclosure was in the center and the assembly lines circulated around it.

Many modern-day designers are lifestyle victims who believe that their inspiration lies solely inside the chic surroundings of their studios, but this kind of thinking is merely an artificial, self-inflicted limitation. Personally, I still draw inspiration from the rhythm of assembly lines and the well-calibrated processes of industrial product assembly. I'm free to imagine what the factory can do for me and what I really can do with the factory. To me, a factory is like a grand piano in its potential for giving life to creativity. We aren't limited to just tapping out one note at a time—we can play real music, if we know our instrument.

The sad truth is that the icons of the Western electronics industry are the ones who have initiated and driven the migration of labor to lower-cost countries around the world, and now the industry and its manufacturers are totally dependent on outsourcing. (The one exception is Japan, which has been underestimated for its industrial prowess and strategic mindset for way too long.) In his brutally pessimistic book, *The Hollowing of America,* James A. Cunningham describes how many high-tech consumer icons—including Motorola, Apple, HP, Dell, and Kodak—have become mere distribution companies of Asian-made products. Cunningham's book, written in 2006, goes on to detail the shrinking of America's manufacturing jobs and productive output and to project a major economic and social crisis for the United States. Today, we've seen that crisis unfold, and its repercussions have been felt around the world. It's important that we all understand both the source and the costs of a depleted manufacturing culture—and that those costs involve lost expertise, not just lost jobs.

Lost Opportunities for Innovation

The single biggest perceived economic advantage to outsourcing or offshoring product manufacturing is lower cost, but achieving dramatically low costs typically requires fractioned, disjointed processes that result in lower quality, higher costs, and limited innovation. To understand this hidden cost, let's begin by looking at the limitations of developing a product for outsourced manufacturing.

First, the product development process (which includes software) has to be efficient. Tasks have to be carefully defined, and things like required features, performance benchmarks, schedule, and budget have to be monitored ruthlessly. While this approach seems fairly logical, in fact, it requires that even early stages of the process include full documentation, with all specs completely listed. Very little interaction between developers and manufacturers is possible, because any interaction may cause a "change of scope," and that could raise the development costs.

Finally, all of the extra effort spent on early-stage documentation, control, and verification detracts from the *essential* work of developing a strong product. This is the development process at its worst—and most costly.

The manufacturing of portable computers is particularly susceptible to this kind of disjointed development and penny pinching. No current original equipment manufacturer (OEM) market leader—aside from Apple—has a strategically unified lineup of accessories such as power supplies, cables, and headphones for their computers, and that's because (1) they don't want to spend the money and (2) they're locked into the manufacturing process of their outsourcing factory partner. If an OEM wants to have standardized accessories, they have to spend time and

asking the tough questions

If a company is considering offshoring or outsourcing (typically, the better of these two choices), there are several questions its leadership should ask before taking the leap:

- **What can you do to improve your business at home?** Maybe you don't need outsourcing to "fix" your problems. Exporting broken processes or a bad corporate culture is a recipe for economic and competitive disaster.

- **Do the numbers really add up? And are you prepared for a long-term battle based on them?** Carefully consider the costs you're taking on with this outside contract. If you are hoping that outsourcing will give you a competitive edge, you have to be prepared to do a stellar job of succeeding with this strategy in the long term, because many of your competitors are doing the same thing.

- **Does your existing workforce support this decision?** Without positive support from your current organization and its "mother lode" of workplace experience and on-site job skills, any outside venture is fragile.

- **Are you familiar (and comfortable) with the laws and governmental structures of the foreign location you're considering for an offshoring operation?** You can't answer these questions from behind your desk in the home office. You'll need to travel to the country and talk to the residents, officials, and business peers who live and work there.

money getting their ODMs and suppliers on the same page with schedul-ing and with internal standards. And that means—gasp!—collaboration. Apple takes on this extra effort, but others do not.

Another "dirty secret" of mismanaged outsourcing is that OEMs and brand owners often waste the opportunity to benefit from the added value that could be delivered by the ODMs they contract with. That's because the OEMs want to keep tight control over the purchasing process and budgets. Some market leaders owe much of their competitive advan-tage to their purchasing and supply chain management. As a hypotheti-cal example, let's say that Dell specs its next-generation notebooks to three or four ODMs in China, with a plan to reward the business to at

- **What is the outlook on environmental practices and security? Can you strike a good balance?** The costs and risks increase for businesses jug-gling global logistics, and so does the ecological responsibility. If the coun-try you're considering as an offshore site doesn't enforce environmental protection laws, you'll have to self-police your carbon emissions, energy consumption, and release of pollutants, if you want to remain a responsible and viable business in the long term.

- **Can you "partner" with the local culture?** You aren't just partnering with foreign factory owners, you're inserting your business into a foreign culture. To find out how well that aspect of the partnership might work, take some of your own people and spend time there in "real life"—attending sports events, eating out, going to the theater, attending concerts, and learning about local politics.

- **Does this arrangement open up a new regional market to you? Can you gain potential by additional growth?** Arrangements that result in more than just reduced production costs lower the risks of offshoring and outsourcing.

- **Is this a strategic move that's likely to bring you a long-term com-petitive advantage?** You have to try to imagine what the future of this relationship will bring before you put the wheels of the deal in motion, because applying the brakes later will be very difficult.

least two of them. Dell's request for bids would list certain components—chip sets, memories, batteries, and displays, for example—that it will purchase directly. At first glance, this direct-purchase strategy might seem to be a good idea, because it avoids one source of overhead. But these parts amount to about 70 percent of a notebook's cost, so this arrangement leaves the ODM very little to work with in putting together a competitive bid. And in many cases, OEMs require "open books," which means that the ODMs lose control of their profits. I even know of deals in which the ODM has been forced to carry a "guaranteed" loss for some time in order to become a major vendor.

But these aren't the most serious losses of fractioned development processes. All good ODMs, such as Foxconn, Wistron, Inventec, Quanta, or Mitec, have strong engineering capabilities. They're not only capable of improving an existing spec, but they actually may be able to design and engineer a better computer overall, and to do it at a lower cost. But given the economic and procedural practice of requisition, the ODMs could actually harm their businesses by offering these improvements to their clients. With lower costs, the ODM would reduce its revenue, along with those of sub-vendors controlled by the OEM. And by improving a client's design, the ODM runs the risk of making enemies with the client's R&D department.

In other words, the fractioned processes used by most OEMs in developing products for outsourced or offshored manufacturing result in diminishing—if not eliminating—the savings these companies might gain by sending their manufacturing work overseas.

Lost Economic Stability

Low cost and low wages, a productive political and educational system supporting economic growth, and a favorable geographic location attract investors and customers. This is exactly the formula capital investors, who always strive for the highest expected return and the lowest presumed risk, are looking for. This formula applies to China, India, and (surprisingly) Eastern Europe today, just as it applied to Singapore in the 1980s. But migrating major manufacturing operations from one community to another (or, in offshoring, from one country to another) sets off an ebb and flow of economic instability that can have a deep and far-reaching impact.

Let's consider one example, that of Nokia, which announced in early 2008 that it would move its German factory—which was highly profitable, but not profitable enough—to Cluj in Romania. Cluj has a well-reputed technical university, whose engineering graduates are willing to work for less than a quarter of the salaries demanded by Western Europeans. Nokia's overall investment in the move was a puny $90 million, but, of course, it also will be transferring its high-tech know-how to tiny Cluj.

The Romanians are well aware that Nokia won't stay. Eventually, local costs and wages will rise, and the Romanians fully expect that, when that happens, the company will move on. A major Bucharest newspaper characterized the agreement with Nokia as a "deal with the locusts" and projected that Nokia will desert the Cluj complex after about ten years. The newspaper's editors reminded readers of the way Nokia treated its German factory towns and workers and urged their Romanian leaders "to drain Nokia dry" before the company does the same to Cluj. One strategy the newspaper editors proposed was to set up separate facilities that mirror Nokia's, and then to invite Western specialists to come in and capitalize on them. This example demonstrates that the economic game has entered a phase in which all participants fully understand the brutal realities of today's global business. But it also illustrates the waves of economic instability that can be created by outsourcing.

Of course, in some regions outsourcing or offshoring actually contribute to economic stability. Mexico is a prime location for American manufacturers who operate facilities under their own names and management, using Mexican facilities and labor. Flextronics, for example, operates a fantastic industrial park in Guadalajara. Another example is the sometimes complicated but still very successful regional collaboration between Japan, Korea, and China. In general, manufacturing thrives best in countries and regions with a qualified history in manufacturing, the right kind of positive ambitions, and close ties to the markets. But when outsourcing is merely an economics-driven, short-term "sacking" of local labor and resources, it up-ends the local economies on both sides of the deal.

Of course, the global economy is driven by multinational companies and micro-economies—such as those in China around Shanghai, Shenzen, Hong Kong, and Macau. In the best of these arrangements, national policies provide political and economic stability and meaningful regulatory guidelines. This certainly is true of India, where the outsourcing and offshoring boom started with clusters of software service companies and eventually included satellite R&D centers for most major software producers, from Microsoft to SAP. In fact, frog's parent company, Aricent, has its center in Delhi. India's outsourcing and offshoring economy contributes just about 16 to 18 percent of India's overall production, but that figure may grow. As wages and labor costs in China have increased, however, India has begun the move into hardware manufacturing. Flextronics already has established a state-of-the-art industrial park in Chennai, planned to occupy eight million square feet.

So, yes, sometimes the whole world benefits from the economic migration of outsourcing and offshoring, through the development of education, infrastructure, and economic opportunity in countries where those things were previously in short supply or even non-existent. On the other hand, those benefits can be short-lived, only to be replaced with problems when the companies end their outsourcing contracts or when labor costs and regulations advance to the point of changing the economic equation. And the benefits of outsourcing and offshoring never come without costs—and sometimes those costs can be substantial.

Adding It All Up

Outsourcing and offshoring may be considered a sound economic strategy by some analysts and institutional shareholders—according to Gartner Research, 80 percent of companies cite cost-cutting as the main reason for outsourcing—but as we've seen, the numbers might not add up to real savings.

If a company really accounted for all expenses associated with the switch to offshoring, for example—including the loss of productivity and loss of revenues during the transfer, the currency exchange rates, the lack of experienced local labor, and the increased wages and salaries required to bring in such labor from the United States—the executives and their public audience would see the true costs of "cheap" labor. Then there's the issue of political and economic stability as well as the time and resources required to navigate foreign administrative regulations—which can be major obstacles for permits. In short, offshoring ventures can end up being much more difficult, much more complex, and much more expensive than many companies anticipate.

Bear in mind that I believe the problems of the offshoring "strategy" (if we call it that) don't extend to all outsourcing agreements. Sometimes there are clear advantages to outsourcing certain functions. But both outsource and offshore companies have to compete honestly and turn an honest profit on the deal they make with their customers. Businesses can't shift costs between business units and locations to magically transform losses into bogus profits. Instead, the best companies equate good performance with good profits.

Too often, however, the purported savings of offshoring and outsourcing never materialize. That means that most of the effort American businesses invest in shifting their manufacturing operations abroad is not only a waste, but it's also a major drag on American businesses, the American economy, and on the very fabric of our national workforce. And we shouldn't underestimate the long and damaging demoralization of losing your job to this losing proposition. More than one company in Western Europe and the United States has forced its local employees to train the outside workers who will take their jobs, before firing those local workers and deserting them and their community. In my opinion, and for all of the reasons I've just outlined, most economically motivated offshoring and outsourcing ventures never should have been pursued in the first place.

But what are our alternatives? Although, as I mentioned earlier, offshoring and outsourcing have come to dominate the manufacturing model, some new, more innovative, and much more sustainable movements are growing. I've seen some of these in action, and I've seen others in the earliest stages of their development. Each of them offers some real and viable alternatives for a more economically and environmentally sound approach to manufacturing.

◦ smart-sourcing: making the most of outside resources

When Steve Jobs went back to Apple in 1996, he asked me for some advice on strengthening the brand's appeal to consumers, and I said, "In principle, it's all about experiences—but they must be *complete* experiences." Apple's iPod-iTunes strategy is a good example of this idea in action. In short, the basic question designers and the companies they work for must consider is "How do we create products that offer a unique and holistic experience?" The more challenging question is, "How do we hit that goal when our factories are located in China, India, or Romania?" And the answer to *that* question is to move to a model of smart-sourcing, versus outsourcing.

Smart-sourcing requires more craft and ingenuity than merely shipping work out to foreign shores to cut production costs. It requires a new development model that includes cross-organizational collaboration early in the process. It also involves a new economic model, because the economics of outsourcing hurt both sides of the partnership. Western brand owners get mediocre products that they have to discount to make them attractive to consumers. ODMs have to live with a lousy profit margin. In smart-sourcing, up-front investments in cross-organizational collaboration result in stronger, more innovative products with greater long-term profitability.

To understand the benefits of smart-sourcing, the big players that dominate the notebook computer market—such as HP, Dell, Acer, Fujitsu, Sony, and Apple—might take some cues from the tiny Swiss start-up Dreamcom and its twenty-five-year-old founding CEO, Janis Widmer. My wife (and business partner) Patricia and I have been so impressed with the company's work and spending ethic that we invested in it. Then, in 2007, we sat down and helped Dreamcom create something that's going to change the game in notebook manufacturing. Our experience offers a good overview of the smart-sourcing model.

After careful consideration, we determined that the most effective and positive innovation we could bring to laptop design was in the area of ergonomics. We created a laptop design that includes a display that can be adjusted to a more ergonomically correct position and a docking module that also improves the laptop's ergonomics, while housing all of its necessary technology extensions in a simple, clutter-free form. We also worked to keep the computer's price as low as possible. In other words, we targeted our efforts at developing a holistic user experience.

From the beginning, it was clear that Dreamcom had to buy its notebooks from an ODM in Taiwan or China. At the same time, we also knew that we couldn't afford to develop a completely new product with the desired innovations and then just pay some ODM to build it. We understood that the ODMs are capable of cutting-edge electronic innovation— which, in most cases, means to compress the most advanced electronics into the smallest possible space. We had only to look at the products Foxconn and Inventec manufacture for Apple to see how extreme this compression can be. It seemed only logical to us that engineers who could create the micro-mechanics of magnetic hard drives should be able to engineer an extendable display mechanism capable of handling the daily routines of work life.

So we decided to approach the ODMs right up-front. We asked a number of ODM leaders to meet with us to discuss our ideas, look over our illustrations, explore the ergonomic demands of the design, and outline our business model. Some weren't interested, but three were quite willing to engage in such an early discussion. Cost wasn't the dominant issue, because by now we were sure that, even with its added functionality, our laptop's cost would be quite competitive. Eventually, Dreamcom decided to go with Wistron, because its executives understood and liked the potential of our project and because the company had a great team of engineers in electronics and micro-mechanics. With this early collaboration, we had leap-frogged over one entire stage of the traditional outsourcing process.

Then our more formal collaboration started. We designed the product together with the ODM's engineers, exchanging files on an almost daily basis via secure servers. This process enabled Jannis Widmer—who is a technical wizard in computing—to develop his radically new product with a team located halfway around the globe, yet still enjoy the same immediacy and synergy of colleagues sharing the same office space. This is one of the more important conditions of successful smart-sourcing: All stakeholders in the project must fully participate and collaborate.

Now came the fun part for me—working together with the Wistron team. They really pushed the envelope and so did I. We looked at different mechanical solutions and at various options for packaging the electronics. We did away with the old-fashioned "tray-loader" CD/DVD drive and implemented an elegant slot-loading drive, and we optimized the feature sets between the notebook and the docking module. We also simplified the user experience by providing a very intuitive analog user interface above the keyboard.

Wistron had control of all technical aspects of the project, and they made very good decisions early on. As we worked on the concept development, Wistron's team really went deep in finding the best vendors in Taiwan and China for parts, surfaces, and special components. Naturally, this level of planning took time and a lot of trial-and-error learning. Even though we went over our original schedule by a couple of months, Wistron delivered such strong results in the prototype stage that we saved the frustration and expense of having to go back and correct problems that typically crop up in the first rounds of production (remember ITT's experience with the portable radios?). Through it all, Jannis Widmer's feedback kept everybody involved in the project excited and motivated to succeed. Overall, this experience was very different from the typical slash-and-burn approach of outsourcing. In developing the first notebooks whose ergonomics met the legal requirements of a regulated European working environment, we put quality and function ahead of shaving the development schedule and pinching pennies.

We launched our new design at the Hannover CeBIT trade show in March of 2008. Dreamcom came out of CeBIT having won wide approval for creating the world's first ergonomic notebook computer, but the audience knew little of the underlying development and business process behind our success. When the manager of a competing company asked me, "How did you get the Taiwanese to produce such a cool product?"

my answer was: "Nobody but the Taiwanese *could* have done it." That's the important message about smart-sourcing. Working with outside partners offers much more tangible—and long-term—rewards when we learn to look beyond the surface benefits of reduced manufacturing costs. When the collaborative process is begun early and managed wisely, ODMs can bring unique benefits to the manufacturing partnership. We just have to be smart enough to leverage them.

For small or mid-size companies, giving away their know-how to ODMs abroad isn't an acceptable strategy, unless they have some hope of reaping large-scale economic benefits from doing so. No amount of outsourcing will help a smaller company "beat" the price of its larger rivals, and smaller companies can't afford to suffer the bad publicity and poor public reaction that outsourcing often triggers. Wall Street is starting to understand the benefits of a sound long-term strategy, even as it smells potential profitability in "green" business innovations. In this environment, small and mid-size companies have to rely on true innovation for their competitive advantage—the type of innovation we launched at Dreamcom—which includes the use of smarter, not just cheaper, labor.

○ home-sourcing: local keys to global rewards

A brand is defined by a product—physical and/or virtual—and the experience customers have with that product. If the experience isn't positive, there is no brand value. But you can't say, "Okay, let's design a gorgeous-looking brand and then let it convey our identity." That's not how brands work. If you need proof of that, consider the companies that have relatively "un-gorgeous" products—for example, Volvo, Dell, and Crocs—but are nevertheless good, strong brands because the companies behind them stick to their strategic goals and deliver on their core strengths. And there's no better way for a small or mid-size company to build (and build on) its brand than through the cultivation of a uniquely talented and loyal workforce—people who understand the brand's strategic goals, are proud of their company's core strengths, and are dedicated to turning out products with a well-defined and superior customer experience.

If a company wants to establish a local identity advantage, it has to be smarter about the way it makes high-end products, and it has to manage them carefully through every step of the PLM chain. To succeed in a competitive marketplace loaded with large-scale manufacturers, small and mid-size companies need an adaptive business and sourcing strategy that I call *home-sourcing*. The home-sourcing strategy combines the advantages of local talent and its unique capabilities with those of globally available product components, to result in truly innovative, unique, *and* economically competitive products.

So what are the objectives for home-sourcing? Economically, a company needs to strike a healthy balance between those production elements that it must source from abroad and those that it can and must cultivate "at home." To decide what elements will fall into each of those categories, company leaders must be guided by the special value their organization can provide. Rather than shooting for some generic product that, in the end, offers little to attract anyone, companies can target their efforts at providing the best possible product for the customers they know best. And nobody knows local users better than a local company.

Home-sourcing benefits companies *and* consumers, and it can provide job security to a local workforce. If a company's local executives, designers/developers, and workers produce something more original and profitable than the generic, mass-marketed dreck that clogs the marketplace, their jobs—in Germany or the United States or wherever—will be safe. In fact, their work may be in demand, because customers love well-made, well-designed products. And the success of home-sourced products and processes may extend well beyond the local marketplace. My client KaVo became a global leader in dental systems after it introduced its innovative and unique new system design.

The German home appliance maker Miele offers another great example of the importance of local sensibilities and talent in creating products that succeed in the global marketplace. German people are known for their love of cleanliness and their sensitivity to environmental issues. They want a washing machine, therefore, that gets their laundry impeccably clean but uses as little water, detergent, and energy as possible. And because many Germans have small homes, the machine also needs to be very quiet. Miele's German designers and engineers succeeded in creating a product that meets all of these "native" imperatives—and, in the process, they have designed a product that is popular around the world. We have a Miele washer and dryer here in California, where water is scarce, electricity is expensive, and the Bay is threatened by pollutants. In Miele's case, as in the case of many companies that have benefited from home-sourcing, the fine-tuning of product design and manufacturing is done best locally. Components such as electronics, motors, and pumps can be sourced anywhere—as long as they meet the quality criteria.

Real home-sourcing starts with an assessment of a company's "native" capabilities and of the available component vendors at home and abroad. Company leaders also have to look at the smartest options for managing a very sophisticated design and manufacturing process. Because home-sourcing affords companies much more freedom in regard to product strategy and close-to-market customization, it's also a good idea to scout online professional blogs and social networks for information about the more exotic trends and detailed customer wishes within the marketplace. And in every detail, companies must maintain impeccable standards for quality, innovation, and personal originality.

Home-sourcing is part of an overall long-range strategy for success, and progress toward strategic goals can seem to move at a snail's pace. Fortunately, I have a "lab" for projecting and testing future results, and that lab is my class at University of Applied Arts in Vienna, Austria. Each semester, we adopt a central theme for student projects, and in 2008, our theme was home sourcing. In exploring that theme, we conducted collaborative workshops with local and global companies. One of these companies, Vienna's legendary piano-maker, Boesendorfer, offered especially interesting opportunities for home-sourced innovation.

Our goal was to create a design that drew upon Boesendorfer's historic and native roots while firmly establishing the company as a forward-thinking, innovative brand. We began by determining which components of the piano were "generic" and which were vital to its individual musical DNA (in the process, we learned that Boesendorfer manufactures everything, including its strings, in-house). We also looked at other examples of classical instrument updates, such as the electric Gibson and Fender

Stratocaster guitars. We studied the convergence of classical music with digital media and learning methods and, finally, we explored new ways of marketing in the domain of true art.

At one point during this process, Ferdinand Braeu, Boesendorfer's director of product development, commented that some pop musicians, such as Robbie Williams, stand while playing the piano. Inspired by that idea, one of our teams created what we dubbed the "transformer piano." The piano was height-adjustable and could be folded up into the shape of a credenza for easy storage—a design that would work well on concert stages and also in smaller homes. Our design gave Boesendorfer's "Made in Vienna" claim true meaning and resonance, as it carried on the tradition of innovation, art, and design for which the city is so famous. Our design demonstrated to Boesendorfer how the company could make products that appeal strongly to Viennese buyers and, at the same time, have global marketability. That kind of success is a realizable goal for any home-sourcing venture. By combining the strengths of the local workforce, traditions, and other native resources with those of carefully chosen "outside" resources, home-sourcing enables companies to produce high-quality, innovative products that will bring them increased market share at home—and abroad.

o personal-fab: building our own brands

We have the industrial revolution to thank for all those deeply discounted, mass-manufactured imported goods that fill the shelves of our big-box stores. But now, with the increased costs, environmental damage, and health risks associated with many low-quality imported goods, the manufacturing pendulum is swinging back in favor of local production. And sometimes, that production can be personal, not just local. In fact, personal manufacturing might be the wave of the future.

One pioneer within this new movement is MIT professor Neil Gershenfeld, who created the concept of desk-top manufacturing, which he calls "Fab Lab." A Fab Lab is basically a low-cost desktop manufacturing "shop" equipped with analog and digital 3D tools and machinery, which is enhanced—and can be globally networked—by computers and digital software. Using a Fab Lab, people can design products for manufacturing right in their own homes and, using a field lab, even participate in building them—and these can be high-quality products, too.

Neil Gershenfeld has set up his Fab Labs in communities around the world and the results are impressive. Fab Lab products range from high-tech components for computers to toys, musical instruments, and personal objects such as eyewear. Gershenfeld makes a credible case that the direct connection between people and the industrial process teaches people new skills, helps to create new jobs, and eventually leads to a more creative and inventive community. This movement has spurred the growth of a number of hybrid business models. Some online businesses, for example, provide customers with basic software for designing an object and then build the object according to the customer's design specifications and ship it off to them.

This model is still in its early stages, of course, and many people realize that designing and manufacturing a workable product for everyday use requires more than just a bit of doodling with a piece of CAD software. Ultimately, the trend toward personal manufacturing will help people develop new competencies. The movement could result in a growing number of students with a basic design vocabulary who are able to visually evaluate designs and draft their own—some will even become true designers. And this is good news. Creative students frequently fail to follow the average "curve" and their talents require special attention and mentoring. Personal fabrication experience could help provide some of the creative exercise that many schools today don't—or can't—offer.

Our world needs all of the enthusiastically creative and talented young people we can muster—perhaps now, more than ever. As we move from the service economy to the creative economy, a healthy population of people with a sound education in both the practical and creative arts is vital for the future success of every region of every country on the planet. Localized, personal production will promote a higher interest in design and other creative professions, while helping those professions take their rightful place in a diverse and evolving economy—and in both local and global markets.

○ the rise of sustainable manufacturing

Our global system is complex and highly unpredictable, but we're foolish not to consider social developments and emerging geopolitical trends. One of the strongest of these developing trends is a growing backlash against the effectiveness of the "economics of efficiency" manufacturing model. For too many years, global business has been mostly driven by perceived economic advantages of "globalization." But the realities of globalization are much different than those perceptions.

Today, even as the capital investment in factories escalates into the billions, when most business analysts talk about "attractive economic conditions" what they're really talking about is low labor costs. So what about the "win/win" benefits of this arrangement? While developing countries sometimes benefit from increased employment and an influx of foreign investment, Western workers—and Western economies—don't fare so well. When all of the highly skilled and qualified jobs have been off-shored or outsourced, the remaining jobs available "at home" are mostly low-paying and low-skilled. This development not only dismantles the backbone of any economy—the spending power of a highly qualified and motivated workforce—but it also deflates the nation's future by taking away the hopes and aspirations of its young people.

As economies in every sector of the developing world shudder and contract under the strain of under-regulated global markets, poorly managed industrialization, and rapidly escalating environmental degradation, many of us are asking the question, "What do we do?" And one important answer to that question lies in a shift toward a more sustainable economic and industrial production model. Around the globe, there is a growing realization that the untrammeled exploitation of human resources and valuable cultural assets isn't possible to sustain. And despite all of the current "bloviators" who tell us that populism is little more than a political fad, most of us sense a major shift in people's consciousness. This game has to change—people don't want to work themselves to exhaustion just to stay afloat. They want to live a more human life.

The demand for increased environmental protection also is pushing the world to adopt a more sustainable manufacturing model. Just consider the wasteful material flow resulting from outsourcing and offshoring: Finished products built in China and India are shipped to the United States and Europe, where they're reshipped around those nations to reach local markets, where they're purchased, used, and then shipped again— either as recycling or just plain trash—back to China, or maybe even on to Africa. How logical—not to mention environmentally sound—is that process? The European Union now requires the OEMs or the "brands" to take back their electronic products (even automobiles), so reverse logistics has become a part of the product lifecycle management. Adding this step in the PLM costs some up-front money, but it also offers new opportunities for innovation.

I see the "economics of efficiency model" struggling on for a while, as companies continue to migrate manufacturing to countries and regions with the lowest wages and the most appealing economic conditions. But I suspect it won't be long before rising market globalization, energy costs, and environmental regulation mean that there won't be any "low-cost" country or region left. While the current model holds, product quality and performance may make sporadic improvements, but overall product culture and innovation will continue to suffer. The risk of exposure to economic downturns or power shifts in global geo-politics is very high for any industry today, and especially threatening to businesses relying solely on offshoring. This model demands scale, and the amount of "product" required to support it will have to increase as already razor-thin margins get squeezed even tighter.

The sustainable manufacturing model is a natural extension of the "only the best" principle that drives all successful corporate models. Sustainable manufacturing results in more holistic product lifecycle management. It also reconnects the factories with consumers and takes advantage of the currently dormant potential of our factories for developing innovation and global product culture. The sustainable manufacturing model is driven by interconnected processes across continents—such as smart-sourcing and home-sourcing solutions. And, because this model is connected more directly to consumers, it's less prone to disruption from economic or political crises.

Right now, economic, political, and environmental conditions offer a unique moment for the move to sustainable manufacturing. Of course, marketers, engineers, designers, and business leaders have to meet the challenge of recognizing this historic opportunity and acting on it. The sustainable manufacturing model represents a true long-term economic strategy. And it works. According to public reports for the fourth quarter of 2008, Apple—a company that largely follows this model—earned more than twice Dell's profits, while pulling in just a little more than 60 percent of Dell's revenues. And the model's profits will extend to both sides of smart-sourcing relationships. Innovation-minded ODMs such as Wistron or Inventec will be big winners.

Of course, we can anticipate vast technological progress in the move toward more intelligent production, whether in the form of refined and fully programmable mechatronics automation and robotics, or new smart and even "living" nano materials. In any case, the factory will become one of the key arenas for the unfolding story of artificial intelligence. But no matter how much manufacturing changes or how far developing trends push it toward globalization or localization, we business leaders, designers, and manufacturers must continually work to find the answer to the same, unwavering questions: How can we make the best use of the manufacturing resources we have available to us, and how can we improve those resources? Only by remaining open to the possibilities—and responsibilities—that accompany that challenge can we hope to find the sustainable success necessary to carry our hopes, dreams, and professional aspirations into the future.

epilogue
already here—and tomorrow

A famous Zen Koan asks: "What is essential about the past, the present, and the future?"—and the answer is "Already here and tomorrow." To me, that Koan teaches that the past and present are our life, but tomorrow is our opportunity. As a realistic optimist, I believe in a better future. And, even though this book is filled with experiences from the past, I hope that it inspires readers to look ahead.

In my role as a mentor, I'm often asked what it was like for young designers back when I first started my own firm. My honest answer is, "Not as good as it is today!" We had to work fanatically for our very survival, and channeling our energy to form a successful team involved a long trial with a lot of errors. But what I remember most about those early days is the lack of clout we designers had with business executives and entrepreneurs. I wasn't willing to play the part of the marginalized "cultural mentor," and so I've spent my career working to build professional partnerships and to establish design's strategic role in business. Today, my goal is to make design the vanguard of humanistic progress and to encourage everyone, no matter what professional and personal paths he or she travels, to share my passion for improving the world. I hope that this book—either by encouraging agreement or by fueling productive debate—will motivate and inspire you to take part in the many positive changes taking place in the world of business, design, manufacturing, and culture.

In the larger context of creativity, design is the living link between our human goals and needs and the material culture that helps to fulfill them. Designers and their business partners have an almost unparalleled opportunity to build an environment that's not only livable and sustainable, but also fun and culturally inspiring. Our material culture is manmade—every component of it is manufactured, sold, used, discarded, and (ideally) recycled and reused. And in every phase of that process, in some way, human ideas are shaped into designs, and designs are manufactured into physical and virtual matter. To build a material culture that uplifts and sustains us, we have to remain ever alert to the opportunities—and sometimes dangerous temptations—of our business models, our strategies, our tools, our processes, and our factories.

Traditionally, ecology hasn't rated high in the value perception of many financially minded people, but that's changing. Bio-fuels are beginning to liberate us from Big Oil, and solar and wind energy technologies are making inroads into the traditional coal-fired energy sector. The Internet is unraveling the old telecommunications companies' hold on customers. And, as we've learned, more companies are adopting sustainable strategic goals and building business models based on long-term vision and ongoing innovation. The old monopolies are falling, and creative endeavors are on the rise.

We still have work to do, however. We need to envision and design a more intelligent and ecological industrial model of production, product support, and recycling. And our solutions can't stop with good product designs. Outsourcing our designs to be produced elsewhere doesn't eliminate our responsibility for the pollution and other negative outcomes of that production, just as we can't take care of our own trash problem by tossing it in our neighbor's yard. The out-of-sight, out-of-mind paradigm must shift, if we want to be responsible industrial citizens.

I believe we have a philosophical obligation to strive for a better world. We have to create a more human-centric conscience in science and business by rethinking our objectives. By adopting positive—and sometimes quite challenging—principles aimed at social accountability and conservation, the benefits of our business efforts can extend beyond the "bottom line" to improve the lives of our families, friends, neighbors, and people around the world. Businesses that work toward those objectives will help to reverse the destruction of the planet—and, ultimately, the money will follow.

As a designer, I'm especially happy when I realize that this new business paradigm will promote livelier, lovelier, and more emotionally fulfilling products. A more appealing product culture will actually be part of a winning green strategy, and this will be true for *all* countries and cultures on earth. Humanizing our industries in Europe and the United States involves developing and implementing an ecological ideal. It will enable us to industrialize poorer countries without destroying their identity and culture. A mobile device, designed, produced, sold, used, and recycled in China, won't have to compete with one provided by a modular production model in Central Africa or the Baltics or Brazil. We'll have more opportunities to buy locally and be more closely engaged in the full lifecycle, profits, and costs of our consumable goods.

While I don't believe that all of our current leaders in politics and business can or will change, I am *quite* optimistic that we, as designers, executives, and consumers, are ready to be mobilized as never before through our understanding of the need for change. We have the most powerful tools for information and influence in history, and they have brought us to the threshold of a new time, driven by new principles and defined by the absolutely urgent need and unlimited opportunity for change. We are poised to extend our influence beyond the borders of bits and atoms and into the very arrangement of neurons and genes, as design enters the realm of advanced scientific research and the augmentation of human performance. As we prepare to enter this vast, new world of creativity in business, science, and industry, our mastery of today's "already here" challenges can guide us as we make "tomorrow" a productive and humanistic adventure. Welcome to the journey!

resources

The following books, articles, and online publications offer interesting perspectives on the topics covered in this book. I encourage you to read them for an even broader understanding of the complex and vital relationships linking business, culture, and design.

Cunningham, J. A. (2006). *The Hollowing of America*. Saratoga, CA: Dark Angel Number Thirteen Publishing Company.

Estridge, P. D. (1984, November). "What Makes a Computer Personal?" *Creative Computing*, 10(11), 194.

Frieberger, P., & Swaine, M. (2000). *Fire in the Valley: The Making of the Personal Computer*. New York: McGraw-Hill.

Gershenfeld, N. (2005) *FAB: The Coming Revolution on Your Desktop—From Personal Computers to Personal Fabrication*. New York: Basic Books.

Gertner, L. V. (2002). *Who Says Elephants Can't Dance?* New York: Harper Business.

Hamel, G. (2002). *Leading the Revolution: How to Thrive in Turbulent Times by Making Innovation a Way of Life*. Cambridge, MA: Harvard Business School Press.

Heiss, J. J. (2003, February 25). "The Future of Virtual Reality: Part Two of a Conversation with Jaron Lanier." *Sun Developer Network* online. http://java.sun.com/features/2003/02/lanier_qa2.html

Illich, I. (1973). *Tools for a Convivial Society*. New York: Harper & Row.

Kawasaki, G. (2004). *The Art of the Start: The Time-Tested, Battle-Hardened Guide for Anyone Starting Anything*. New York: Portfolio.

Kant, Immanuel, with Paul Guyer and Alan Woods (Eds.) (1999). *Critique of Pure Reason* (1781). London: Cambridge University Press.

Kelley, T., & Littman, J. (2005). *The Ten Faces of Innovation: IDEO's Strategies for Defeating the Devil's Advocate and Driving Creativity Throughout Your Organization*. New York: Doubleday Business.

Kidder, T. (2000). *The Soul of a New Machine*. Newport Beach, CA: Back Bay Books.

Ohmae, K. (1991). *The Mind of the Strategist: The Art of Japanese Business*. New York: McGraw-Hill.

Peters, T., & Waterman, R. (2004). *In Search of Excellence: Lessons from America's Best-Run Companies*. New York: Collins Business.

Reardon, M. (2008, October 30). "Motorola's Struggle for Survival." *CNET News* online edition. http://news.cnet.com/8301-1035 _3-10079539-94.html

Roach, S. S. (2004, July 22.) "More Jobs, Worse Work." *The New York Times*.

Rule, A. (2008, January 11). "The Revolution Will Not Be Designed." *In These Times* online magazine. http://www.inthesetimes.com/ article/3464/the_revolution_will_not_be_designed/

Smith, A. (2008). *Theory of Moral Sentiments* (1759). Bibliolife. http:// bibliolife.com/

Smith, A. (2007). *The Wealth of Nations* (orig. 1776). Hampshire, UK: Harriman House.

U.S. House of Representatives Committee on Oversight and Government Reform. (2007, December). *Political Interference with Climate
Change Science Under the Bush Administration.* http://oversight.
house.gov/documents/20071210101633.pdf

index

acknowledgments

It has been hard for me to write the acknowledgments for this book. Everybody was so important. I love the game of soccer—"football" in the rest of the World—so maybe my favorite sport serves as a good analogy. A well-played game is the experience, hard work, and passion of many. I am hoarse after every good game, shouting with jubilant joy or frustration, depending on the flow of the game. The folks at Jossey-Bass were the coaches and managers who put this together: Karen Murphy, Lorna Gentry and their team had the courage to put this book on its path. frog was my Wembley Stadium, the best place on earth for decades—the place where I was allowed to mostly excel, but also experience some defeats. A big "thank you" to Doreen Lorenzo, Mark Rolston, Collin Cole, Bettina Teschner, and so many other players, who ensure that we still keep playing a winning game every day. Tim Leberecht, Sam Martin, Sarah Munday, and the marketing team at frog are great cheerleaders who kept us going.

People who have given us a chance to win are plentiful. All of frog's clients show up to compete in a global competitive environment every day. And my rookies at the University of Applied Art in Vienna are a surprise and a great learning experience every day. I expect lots from them.

Finally, my family is my backbone: A blended global mesh that covers each others' backs, and we all understand what it takes to play together.

Thank you all.

endorsements

"A breath of turbo-charged fresh air that doesn't regurgitate the ego-maniac CEO's selective memory or an outside expert's mis-interpretations. Hartmut explains innovation through the lens of design, and it's about time we gained his valuable perspective."

—**Guy Kawasaki,** former chief evangelist of Apple
and co-founder of Alltop.com

"At Flextronics, we fell in love with Hartmut and frog, and their passion for bringing crazy great designs and design processes into the forefront of great product companies. We used their expertise to help our customers, many of the greatest product companies in the world, including Apple, HP, Cisco, Microsoft and others. It is a credit to Hartmut and his partner Patricia that in the midst of today's shocking global recession, frog is setting quarterly revenue records. Theirs is a unique and fascinating story."

—**Michael Marks,** partner Riverwood Capital LLC
& former CEO, Flextronics

"What a bonus for all of us that Hartmut has put to pen his story of endeavor and achievement and written with such humility. He dared to think and act beyond his profession's defined parameters. He combined his virtues of head and heart and brought humanity to products. His new approach to design is felt in every room in every house in every country and in every business around the world. He proved that thoughtful design is not only good for people but is good for business—and that both are interlinked. I have been fortunate to have observed first hand his impact at Sony, Apple, and HP and have learned so much from him. He is an unsung hero of our times! *A Fine Line* is a must-read for designers and business people alike."

    —**Satjiv Chahil,** senior vice president for Worldwide Marketing, Hewlett-Packard

"A fascinating, breathtaking, and exemplary insight into a success story that never had so much topicality, and so much informative potential as just now. Esslinger offers an honest and encouraging portrait of the incredible power of the business and design alliance. *A Fine Line* is a handbook of design expertise and the art of business at its best, showing a variety of radical solutions and fresh new ideas.

    The book is about listening. About reading between the lines and being sensitive to human needs. About courage and believing in both cultural and economic success, no matter how stony the way to the goal might be. The book talks about building bridges between creative minds and business minds. It stands as an homage to strategic design as a passion and as a profession by the "Che Guevara" of the good form. A must for all business leaders as well as designers."

    —**Professor Dr. Peter Zec,** president, International Council of Societies of Industrial Design (ICSID) and founder, red dot awards

"True to Hartmut Esslinger's visionary self, *A Fine Line* is an excellent commentary on the value of design and design-minded people to our businesses and our societies at large. It's packed with great insights for business people and innovators alike."

—**Thomas Lockwood,** Ph.D., president,
the Design Management Institute

"*A Fine Line* is very enlightening. Design is a magic thing which crosses nations and history, creates value, and improves our life. Hartmut Esslinger is always eager to share and exchange his ideas and experiences with those people who have in their mind clearly what the real purpose of design is. Hartmut is not only the pride of Germany and America, he is also the giant who belongs to the world design community."

—**Yang Zheqing,** CEO, Shanghai Design Biennial & Shanghai Centre for Scientific and Technological Exchange with Foreign Countries (SSTEC)